THE ECOLOGY COOKBOOK

THE ECOLOGY COOKBOOK

AN EARTH MOTHER'S ADVISORY

NAN HOSMER PIPESTEM & JUDI OHR

CELESTIAL ARTS
BERKELEY, CALIFORNIA

Cover and text design by Ken Scott
Cover painting by Nan Pipestem
Composition by Ann Flanagan Typography
Illustrations are from *1800 Woodcuts by Thomas Bewick and His School* © 1962 by Dover Publications.
Used with the kind permission of the publisher.

FIRST PRINTING, 1991

0   9   8   7   6   5   4   3   2   1
95   94   93   92   91

Library of Congress Cataloging-in-Publication Data
Pipestem, Nan Hosmer, 1937–
     The ecology cookbook : an earth mother's advisory / Nan Hosmer
Pipestem & Judi Ohr.
         p.   cm.
     Includes bibliographical references and index.
     ISBN 0-89087-632-0
     1. Cookery (Natural foods)   2. Ecology.   I. Ohr, Judi.
     II. Title.
     TX741.P56   1991
     641.5′63—dc20   90-20425
                                                           CIP

Printed on Recycled Paper

This book is dedicated to survival...

May we always have the tools to perform,
the knowledge necessary to use them,
and the perception to see what needs to be done.

CONTENTS

INTRODUCTION

S elf-sufficiency is still a dream. Not all people can attain it, of course, but it is a goal. The ecological and educational problems of the planet are too acute to be dealt with only through the academic channels of our society. It is up to us to take action *now*. No longer is there time to wait for academicians to influence political leaders with the expectation that something will be done. It truly is up to us.

The Ecology Cookbook has been designed to serve as a guideline. We present the book hoping to expose to people who might not otherwise come into direct contact with them the methods and techniques of survival itself. Nowadays, "Ecology Now" means more than a bumpersticker on a dirty car. Ecology starts with humankind—mind and body. We must re-evaluate our lifestyle on the planet, or the present structure of the planet will not survive.

For centuries man has taken *from* the natural resources of the planet. Now those resources are diminishing. The few that are left are polluted. We have very little time to change our habits of daily living. In writing this book, we have been able to understand humankind's ability to change the planet's destiny. In our writing and research, we hope to influence positively the changing environment in which we live.

The data in this book present an alternative way of living in a slowly diminishing world of imbalance. The object of writing a book on the subject of natural foods and survival concepts is to introduce the reader to the concepts of returning to the real needs of man. We see these needs as: *Food, Shelter, Love and Lots of hope* for a future of balance and harmony on the planet.

Today the concept of eating nutritional quality food and living a lifestyle geared to the resources available has become a way of life for many people. Five years ago we asked our families to observe their daily habits. As time has passed, we have discovered many ways to conserve our resources. It has not been easy for our families and friends to accept many of our new habits of conservation. One of our new habits of conservation was to eliminate flushing the toilet at each urination. As we explained the ecological reasons for this change, our children exploded by saying, "How gross." But time marches on. We learn to adapt, and as another drought season is upon us, we had to adapt. As two separate families living in two separate households here in San Benito County, we live with the limited resources available.

In the fall of 1973, I introduced Natural Foods and Survival Concepts to the curriculum at Gavilan College. The class was designed with the intention of introducing a sensible method of balancing nutritional as well as ecological needs to suit the changes that have occurred in the ecological structure of the planet. Food shortages, as well as shortages of fossil fuels and water, have become obvious. From this beginning *The Ecology Cookbook* has been developed to provide a sensible pattern of living for all. Only the best quality foods are used to prepare the recipes included in the format of this book.

Many people are buying and selling natural foods. Many markets now stock grains and flours that are packaged just as the unrefined commodities of old. Many people are getting on the natural food bandwagon. There is plenty of room for all to enjoy and profit both financially and healthfully from the "return to sensible living." Don't be afraid to take your old standard or traditional recipes and substitute natural food ingredients for the ingredients that contain little nutritional quality.

As we follow a natural diet and incorporate survival methods into our daily habits, we become one with the universe. We understand the basic needs of mankind. Food, shelter, love and hope become household necessities. Sunshine, fresh air, and exercise are other ingredients of healthy living. As we study and experience the natural way of life, we continually re-examine our attitudes toward others. As we share this "organicity" with others, we become aware of the potential balance between man and his environment. As we overcome our self image as epicurean hogs, we learn to yield without resistance. We learn to say "no" to many tempting foods. We learn to live a sensible life filled with moderation and balance.

After many years of research and experimentation, my conclusion is that we must use education as a tool in order to communicate the message of our need for change. As we prepare and hope for a future filled with health and happiness, we conserve, enjoy, and protect the resources that are available to us. We must develop a desire to live within our means—ecologically, biologically and spiritually. Desire is the key word in my survival plan for the future; we must *want* to survive. We must rely on our available resources. "Education is man's greatest commodity."

—Judi Ohr
San Juan Canyon

CHAPTER 1

PROJECTING YOUR OWN MOVIE

Most of us become tired or bored with our images at some time. We become dissatisfied with our bodies and minds. Sometimes we catch ourselves doing the same things, day after day, year after year. We realize that, in order to move ahead, we must change our attitude and habits. Most of us have no desire to feel the drain of boredom and fatigue. We find ourselves caught up in the rat-race of living like robots. We take time out for everything *except* our own individual needs. We make excuses and continue to work with the same attitudes and habits. "When the children are grown up, when we retire, when I am finished with college, when I am older, when I have more time, when I have more energy..."

The fact is, we are lazy. We become people of habit. We have been brain-washed into a slow vegetation. We lack self-control. We have not developed our individual potentials. We have not established our own "way." We have adapted the way of the community. "Everybody eats like this, everybody dresses like that. Everybody around me is doing it." The list is endless.

So what? So everybody is going off to the moon. What do you care? If you have no desire to follow them, if you have no desire to look like them, if you want to "do your own thing," all you have to do is "do it." If you cannot remain composed and calm during an emergency, perhaps you need to reevaluate your position in the environment and develop a sense of control within your own physical and mental body.

1

The system of thinking and projecting your *own* movie will result in an atunement with the environment of people, places, and things around you. The exercises will help you concentrate and relax. You will accomplish your goals on a daily basis. You will not have to "wait" to change your habits and attitudes. As you train the parts of your body to react to your commands, you will unite your body with your spirit. Soon the image you are projecting will become your reality. You will be the controller of your mind and body. As you begin to feel comfortable with your new reality, you will find you can change your reality.

The method of projecting your own movie contains five basic principles:

1. Maintaining a quiet mind in order to allow thoughts to enter;
2. Developing the desire to listen, in order to learn;
3. Developing the desire to remember, in order that we can learn from experiences;
4. Developing a sense of understanding in order to give meaning to our existence;
5. Acting, in order to project the images which will eventually become our "way."

In developing a system that works, we have held onto the concepts of time and space. We realize that time and space meet at a place called *now*. Now is the reality of our existence. As we live each day, we discover that each moment is precious, and we live, in love with living, survival becoming our number one quest.

As we project our *own* movies, we learn to relax and take each day one at a time. We accept what we have and hope to improve. The basic necessities bring us our simple pleasures of life. *Food, Shelter, Love, and lots of hope* provide us with a strong desire to project the movie of our choice. The system of projecting your own movie can work for anyone who wants to change his or her self image. All it takes to project a new movie is the desire to change the old tape.

Change is certain. As we develop the ability to accept what we have no power to control, we change our destiny and create a new self image. Time and space meet at a place called *now*.

CHAPTER 2

HEALTH FOODS, NATURAL FOODS MEAN GOOD NUTRITION

One very important factor we must consider when examining our nutritional intake is individual need. We are all individuals and our needs are not the same. If a food does not agree with you, do not eat it. There is no indispensable food, only indispensable nutrients. Modern humankind created suffering by destroying good foods just as the natural balance in nature has been upset by polluting the environment. We have made only destructive assaults on our food in our attempt at "food-technology" in the last 200 years.

Food refining and processing—polluting the foods with sprays and changing the foods with chemical additives that deceive the consumer—are problems that will be difficult to change. Waste and ignorance are the two factors holding us back from the balance necessary for survival. We have created a natural scandal which may not be easily corrected.

Today, we have food items on the shelves which should not be classified as foods because they contain little "food" in terms of *nutritional* value. Convenience foods are becoming more and more accepted. Foods highest in nutritional value take time to prepare, and many people, driven by their careers only, refuse to spend time in the kitchen.

The quality of our foods is lost in some processing. One good example is a raw potato; by the time it is processed, then reconstituted and made into potato flakes in a can, it has lost 91.4 percent of its vitamin C value. Boiling or baking and eating soon after gives a loss of 20 percent.

Many of the combinations and chemical mixtures cannot really be called food. They deceive the appetite, they lack nutritive value. Many have enough money to supply themselves with the right foods; however, they have no knowledge of the foods necessary for proper nutritional balance.

The following is a guideline to sensible food intake:

1. Buy and use foods that are as near to their natural state as possible. The best way to ensure the highest nutritional quality is to raise it yourself. This is the most valid of all rules.
2. Quality is the most important thing to consider when planning meals. It makes no nutritional sense to serve a large *variety* of foods when our nutritional needs are for foods of high nutritional *quality*.
3. If you do not care for certain foods that are popular and considered nutritionally sound, compensate through the use of foods which will provide the same nutrients.
4. If you are not sure of the nutritional quality of the foods you prepare and eat, take a vitamin supplement for insurance. Remember, the foods should come first; do not expect a supplement to take the place of good quality food.
5. Don't be hassled by differences of opinion. Establish your nutritional needs according to your own requirements. Study and evaluate the various ways and means and adapt them to your own needs. Do not hop from fad to fad; your body will not tolerate the changes very well.
6. Avoid processed foods; take time to prepare wholesome whole foods.
7. Learn to substitute honey for sugar. Use wheat flour in place of refined white flour. Use unbleached flour in place of the bleached flour. Experiment with flours and grains.
8. Avoid foods containing chemical additives. Learn to read labels. If you cannot read a word, don't buy it.
9. Use fresh vegetables daily, home grown whenever possible.
10. Use yogurt or keifer often. Acidophilus is a good substitute.

11. Use wheat germ, nutritional yeast, protein powders as supplements, but do not rely on them as food.
12. Learn to listen to your mind and body. Find your own balance. Learn not to be hard on yourself. If your head craves a food that you know has little nutritional value, treat yourself to it. Nothing is worth the stress abstinence sometimes brings about.

The balance is what feels right to you. There is no rule of measure that fits each of us individually. The trick is to arrive at your own balance, at your own pace, and to maintain that pace until your body and mind give you a sign that it is time for change. Question the quality of the ingredients used in the preparation of your foods. Do not discard your favorite recipes, but learn to adapt your own style of cooking to use good quality ingredients. Our families' health is dependent on the quality of the ingredients we use to prepare our meals.

CHAPTER 3

CALORIES DON'T COUNT— COMMON SENSE DOES

Until we learn to experience our individual control, we cannot develop our individual habits. We must realize the fact that we *do* have control over our subconscious and *use* that control to develop a healthy pattern of living. We cannot continue to accept the patterns and habits of the environment around us. As individuals, we *"know"* more than we want to admit. We know if we are living each day with an attitude of self-development. We *know* if we continue to travel the path of the *"robot"* we will reach the end of the road sooner than necessary. If we travel on a road and there is a sign that reads *detour,* we do not continue on the road. We go around the detour, or we take another path. Should we be so stupid as to think we can continue after having read the warning, we will soon come to the end of the path.

Our bodies give us many signs each day. We must learn to pay attention to the signs. Start today. Begin by taking your clothes off. Now stand in front of the mirror and observe the structure of your body. Know that if you are not pleased with what you see, you have the power to change the structure. In order to change what you see in the mirror, you must have *desire* and *hope*.

You do *not* have to stick with a strict diet in order to lose weight. You do not have to become involved in *fad* diets. You do not have to restrict your body and mind to the point of stress. The stress caused from dieting often causes more harm than the fat on our bodies. We must learn to use common sense. Learn what foods are of the highest nutritional value. Learn to control your nutritional intake. The following are guidelines to a sensible daily regime:

1. Buy foods which are as close to their natural states as possible;
2. Pay more attention to the nutritional intake and less attention to the quantity of the foods you are buying and eating;
3. Do not follow fad diets or crash diets. They tend to cause stress;
4. If you see the need to *give up* a particular food, replace it with one of equal nutritional value. Example: If you decide not to eat meat because of the way it is processed, you must eat foods that contain a good balance of amino acids. Protein is an essential part of every diet;
5. Establish your individual needs according to your own requirements. Study and work at your own pace. Evaluate the various ways and adapt them to your own needs;
6. Avoid processed foods. Learn to read labels. If you cannot read a word, do not buy the item. Calcium nitrate, sodium benzoate, are poisons to your system. Preservatives are the killers of mankind. Eat foods in season. Eat live foods. Eat to live. Do not eat to fill your belly. Think before you say *yes*. Learn to say *no*. Practice quantity control in order to develop *quality* control;
7. Learn to make each day a special day for your own individual body and mind. Direct each day in order to accomplish your own individual goals. Do not be afraid to set high goals. Your own individual desire and hope make any goal *possible;*

8. Learn to listen to your own body and mind. Find your own balance. You have the ability to control your own environment. If you are not happy with the environment, do something to change it or your attitude towards it. Enjoy living each day the best you can.

WORDS OF WARNING!

Even in the health food store—*read labels!* Many brands of tofu have additives or preservatives.

Herbs must be fresh to be good. Dried herbs should have definite fragrance in order to be considered edible. Be sure to sniff! More herb specialty shops are coming into existence. These little places specialize in herbs, herb tea blends and sometimes even coffee.

Pills are not health food. Good vitamins made from natural ingredients may be purchased at your health food store. This doesn't mean you can or should survive on vitamin pills. Any "health food" store that specializes in pills you should avoid like the plague.

BASIC SENSES FOR SHOPPING

1. Common sense—use it!
2. Eye sense—read the labels.
3. Nose sense—use your nose.
4. Taste sense—don't be afraid to ask for a small sample.
5. Feeling—especially fruit—*always be gentle.*
6. Listening—Learn to ask questions of your grocer and listen to his answers.

And remember, no nonsense from these guys—your family's nutrition is important!

CHAPTER 4

SHOPPING SENSE

After all the talk about good food, good nutrition, preservatives, additives, and so on, everyone may wonder, "Where do I begin?" Many good foods are available at your local supermarket—sometimes they are not so easy to find. The most important directive that we can offer is that you *read the label*.

More supermarkets nowadays are stocking natural foods. The label "Natural Food" means there are no additives or preservatives in the product. It does not necessarily mean the food is good for you. Many "natural foods," especially cereal products, contain unhealthy amounts of sugar. Sugar tastes good, but it is *not* good for you. Wheat germ, oatmeal, unbleached flours, some whole grain flours, some yeast, herbs and spices may be safely purchased from your local market. Always take the time to read the label.

Fresh produce (fruits and vegetables) in season is usually a good buy nutritionally. Naturally, home grown produce is the very best, because if you grow your own, you know just exactly what has gone into the plant. Use your eyes, your nose, and your fingers to inspect produce. *Always be gentle,* as bruised fruits and vegetables are not salable.

SHOPPING IN A HEALTH FOOD STORE

Health food stores are mazes for the uninitiated. Crowded, poorly lit, cramped for elbow room, places are all that many of us have seen—certainly not conducive to browsing. Plan your trip! If the health food store nearest you sells bulk commodities, by all means buy bulk.

8

Bulk honey is much cheaper than pre-packaged. Commercial bee people are allowed to cut their honey with as much as 20 percent water and still call it 100 percent pure honey! If you buy bulk honey—no problem—it is thick. Sometimes you can even buy crystalized honey for a good price. In order to "rejuvenate" it, just put the jar of honey in a pan of warm water and place it on the stove over low heat for awhile to liquefy. Other good bulk items to look for are vanilla, carob (a chocolate substitute), shampoo, nut butters (peanut, sesame, cashew), grated coconut, whole grains, dry beans, and herbs. Be sure to take your own containers along for bulk liquid ingredients. (For example, it's impossible to bring your honey home in a paper bag.) Health food stores carry healthful varieties of pasta and an amazing number of seeds to sprout for eating. Good yogurt is available as well as excellent tofu (soy bean curd) and cheese. Both soy sauce and tamari sauce may be purchased in bulk in some health food stores and are free from preservatives. Powdered non-instant dry milk is carried only by health food stores. Most of the instant dried milk stocked by supermarkets contain preservatives so the yogurt produced would not be of benefit to anyone.

CHAPTER 5

GETTING STARTED WITH HEALTH FOODS

Exercise and a diet of whole live food is very important. We must be sure that the food we eat is of the highest nutritional value. In substituting natural ingredients for processed ones, we must remember the reason for substitutions: Processed foods contain little food value. The following are natural food items which can be used in place of those food items already present in our daily diets. This list also contains methods of introducing these foods to the people we are preparing meals for.

❧

BROWN RICE Rice which has been husked still retains the germ and bran that contain the vitamins and minerals our bodies need for development. Brown rice takes longer to prepare than white rice, and it requires more cooking time. This rice can be long or short grain and can be prepared in the same recipes as white rice; just remember that it requires longer cooking time.

❧

RAW SUGAR Less refined than white sugar, it is light brown in color and contains a few minerals; white sugar has none. Eliminate recipes that call for sugar in amounts larger than one cup, as a little goes a long way. (When sugar is processed, most of the calcium is processed out of the sugar in the process of refinement. As the sugar hits the body, it draws calcium from the body.) As for artificial sweeteners—*do not use them, as most of them contain chemicals and are dangerous to the health of the body.*

❧

SEA SALT Salt obtained by the evaporation of sea water which contains minerals. It is used in place of regular salt. May be purchased plain or iodized.

❧

TAHINI A nut butter made from sesame seeds. A good source of phosphorus and fatty acids.

❧

TURBINADO SUGAR Another name for raw sugar.

❧

WHEAT GERM The most valuable part of the wheat kernel. It contains both E and B vitamins. There is no wheat germ in white bread, as the germ has been removed from the flour. Wheat germ must be refrigerated after it has been opened. It can be added to breads in order to increase the nutritional value of the bread. We use ½ cup wheat germ to four cups of flour. You may substitute ½ cup wheat germ for ½ cup flour in any recipe. Try sprinkling it over some fruit or breading with it. We like to use it to bread liver.

❧

WHOLE GRAIN Any grain with its bran and germ intact. The germ and bran contain all the vitamins and minerals.

❧

WHOLE WHEAT A grain that is ground into flour for baking.

YOGURT A food produced by the action of a bactcrial culture on milk. It aids in the production of B vitamins in the body. The bacteria also changes the milk to an acid substance and makes it more digestible. It supplies high protein and B vitamins to the body. It contains a good flora which helps ward off bad germs. In order to maintain the flora in our intestines, we should consider taking some yogurt or acidophilus milk every day. If you are taking antibiotics, it is important to take in this good bacteria every day. The antibiotics destroy the good bacteria in the body, and it must be replaced in order to maintain good health.

BULGUR WHEAT A wheat that has been prepared for cooking by cracking, steaming and toasting. It is sold under the name of "Ala" in many stores. "Ala" may be used in place of rice or pasta.

HONEY Used exclusively by many as a sweetener in cooking and baking. If you are using honey instead of the amount of sugar found in recipes, use ½ the amount of honey as of the sugar called for. Example: one cup sugar, use ½ cup honey.

DRY SKIM MILK One-half cup of powdered milk contains all of the nutrients found in a quart of fresh milk. It contains more food value because it is so highly concentrated. It contains more proteins and is more easily digested than fresh milk. It contains lots of calcium and riboflavin. For years, fresh milk has been said to be a perfect food. How can it be perfect if it is so hard to digest? If there is a problem with allergies or digestion, it would do well to try using powdered dry milk instead. Because of its concentration, it contains eleven times more food value than fresh milk.

SEEDS AND NUTS Seeds contain lots of B and E vitamins. Nuts, legumes and unrefined cereals contain large amounts of B. The unsaturated fatty acids called vitamin F are also found in nuts and seeds. Fats are carried by lecithin in the diet. Lecithin distributes the fats to the parts of the body where it is needed. The two most important elements of nuts and seeds are phosphorus and iron. Both of these elements are destroyed by refining. Do not count on them being in processed foods.

CHAPTER 6

A GUIDE
TO NATURAL
WHOLE GRAIN FLOURS
AND REGULAR FLOURS

All natural foods are denoted by an asterisk.

❧

ARROWROOT Finely ground tuberous rootstocks of the arrowroot. The nutritious starch yielded by this plant may be used in place of corn or tapioca starches. This is the only starch that has an alkaline ash with calcium content. This starch may be added to infant milk to increase the carbohydrate quality.

❧

BARLEY* A finely ground hulled barley for blending with other flours in baking bread, muffins, cakes, hotcakes, and cookies. Use in infant feeding.

❧

BUCKWHEAT* Pure eastern buckwheat flour. Makes great "old time" waffles and hotcakes.

❧

CORN* (whole grain) (yellow) Whole ground from select mideastern corn. Used in breading, hotcakes, and waffles. This corn flour mixes well with other flours.

❧

GARBANZO* Ground from chick peas. Alkaline tendency. Use with other flour.

GARBANZO MEAL* Good made into falafal. Spices are added to ground garbanzo beans.

GLUTEN Low starch flour made by washing the starch from high protein wheat flour. The gluten is dried and ground. When using gluten flour, you may use more rye, soya, or other specialty flours. May be used in baking breads and hotcakes. Good for gravies. Usually exceeds 50 percent protein.

GRAHAM* A whole grain wheat flour ground with the bran layers left intact. This retains a coarse and light textured flour.

LIMA BEAN* A specialty flour ground from lima beans. This flour is used with other flours.

MILLET* Finely ground alkaline easily digestible. Especially good for restricted diets of wheat or rye. High in B2, lecithin, iron, magnesium, calcium, and amino acids.

OAT* (whole grain) Use with other flours in baking muffins, hotcakes and breads. A good substitute in restricted diets.

POTATO* (fine meal) Use in soups, breads, hotcakes, muffins, and gravies. Blend with other flours before adding liquids to prevent lumping. This fine-grind meal must be blended with other flours or dry ingredients before mixing into dough.

POTATO STARCH Finely ground starch made from potatoes. A nutritious starch used as a thickening agent.

RICE* (whole grain brown) Rice reduced to flour for blending with other flours in all baking and breading. Excellent added to waffles and pancakes. One of the flours used in allergy or restricted diets. An excellent flour to make into a batter for breading.

RICE* (white) Polished white rice reduced to flour. Use the same as in brown rice flour.

❖

RICE BRAN (brown) Brown rice reduced to bran. Use to increase the nutritional quality of products.

❖

*RICE POLISHING** (brown) Inner bran layers from brown rice. A by-product made from polishing natural rice into white rice. Contains many vitamins and minerals. Add to foods as you would wheat germ. This increases the nutritional value of the food. A good source of calcium. Easily digested.

❖

*RYE** (whole grain) Dark northern rye. A coarse specialty grind. Use in breads and muffins.

❖

*RYE** (whole grain Pumpernickel) A special ground flour which has a coarse texture.

❖

*SOYA** (whole bean raw) Recommended for home consumption. Soya beans ground into a flour. Produces a nut-like flavor. Increases the nutritional quality of the food.

❖

*SOYA** (low fat or for milk) A fine soya powder which is low in fat, and may be used in place of non-fat dry milk for breads, cookies and drinks.

❖

TAPIOCA A beady starch obtained from the cassava root. Use for puddings and as a thickening agent in cooking.

❖

*TRITICALE** (whole grain) New wheat-rye flour. Ground flour from a grain that is a cross between rye and wheat. Use with other flours.

❖

UNBLEACHED (hard wheat regular) A refined flour from hard wheat. No bleaching, no preserving chemicals have been used in this flour. Use for all purpose baking.

❖

UNBLEACHED (pastry soft wheat) A refined flour from soft wheat. Processed as unbleached hard wheat. Use in cookies, pies, and general pastry.

UNBLEACHED (natural hard wheat)   Used to increase the nutritional quality of products. Use in muffins, breads, and cookies.

WHOLE WHEAT* (whole grain spring)   A whole grain flour milled by a low heat method in order to preserve the full nutritional quality of the grain. This flour is ideal for making breads and other whole wheat products. This flour contains all of the germ and natural minerals. This flour is not recommended for making pastries due to its high gluten content.

WHOLE WHEAT* (whole grain medium)   Flour ground from whole wheat with all the nutritional quality left intact. Nothing is removed, and all the bran and germ is reduced to flour.

WHOLE WHEAT* (whole grain coarse)   A whole grain flour milled by a low heat method in order to preserve the full nutritional quality of the grain. This flour is good to make breads and other whole wheat products. Also not recommended for making pastries due to its high gluten content.

WHOLE WHEAT (whole grain special)   Whole wheat ground in order to preserve the natural quality of the grain.

WHOLE WHEAT (whole grain pastry)   Finely ground soft white pastry wheat. Use to replace all white flour in pastry baking, including pies, waffles, cakes, cookies. You may sift two or three times after measuring to produce a lighter product in pastries.

The following freshly milled meals may be added to your baking products: Chia, Flax, Sesame, Sunflower, Poppy, Red clover (for sprouting), Sunflower (cracked), Sunflower (roasted with sea salt), Alfalfa (for sprouting), Caraway, Fenugreek, Pumpkin, and Radish.

CHAPTER 7

BULK CEREALS AND GRAINS

BARLEY (flakes) Light flakes of natural white barley with only the "hull" or "chaff" removed. A flavorful addition to soups, cereals, and breads.

❧

BARLEY (grits) Whole hulled barley cracked in separate pieces. A nutritional addition to soups, cereals, and loaves. These grits are good meat extenders.

❧

BUCKWHEAT GROATS (toasted brown) Whole toasted buckwheat used for cereals, soup, pudding, and stuffing.

❧

BUCKWHEAT GROATS (white raw) Whole buckwheat that can be used for pancakes, stuffing, soup, and cereals.

❧

CEREAL (nine grain) Contains all natural grains, nothing has been removed. A combination of nine grains: wheat, oats, corn, barley, rye, rice, soya, millet, flax seed, and triticale. A nutritious addition to breads and cookies. Nutritious and hearty when cooked as a breakfast cereal.

❧

CEREAL (four grains) A combination of wheat, barley, oats, and rye. This cereal may be added to breads and cookies as well as muffins. An excellent breakfast dish when served with honey and milk. This is a lightly flaked cereal.

❧

CORN (whole yellow) For grinding, offered in various grinds.

CORN MEAL (stone ground regular) Stone ground from select corn to a medium meal consistency. All of the corn germ is left intact. Use in combination with other flours to produce cornbread, muffins, hotcakes, and bread.

❧

CORN MEAL (fine) Corn which has been ground to a fine texture. Use in combination with other flours in breads, muffins, and hotcakes. Delicious when cooked as a cereal. May be added to casserole dishes. Also use in breading and batters.

❧

CORN MEAL (coarse—Polenta) A coarse meal ground from select yellow corn. Ground for use in casserole dishes. Excellent cooked as a "mush." This corn has not been de-germinated.

❧

MILLET (popcorn) Highest quality corn. Pops tender and large.

❧

MILLET (whole hulled) Freshly hulled millet. Alkaline forming, easy to digest. This grain can be steamed light and fluffy for delicious casseroles, puddings, and cereals. This grain is a good source of protein. May be used as a meat extender.

❧

MILLET (grits) Broken bits of millet. Millet is a good source of calcium and lecithin. May be used as a side dish, cereal, in soups, and breads.

❧

MILLET (meal) Medium grind from hulled grain. Use with equal parts of corn meal in dishes as tamale pie, mush, for cereal, and for frying. The unusually high quality of millet protein and lecithin make it a good meat extender.

❧

OATS (old fashioned steam rolled) Large separate flakes. Cooks into large flakes. Use for cooking, cereal, and cakes. You may toast in the oven for added flavor. A lightly steamed whole oat which is flattened to be used in cookies, breads, and muffins. This grain takes a little longer to cook.

❧

OATS (quick) Half the size of flake. A smaller oat flake. This grain cooks in less time. This grain is more delicate than whole oats. Use as a cereal and as an addition to breads and cookies.

ॐ

OATS (steel cut) A steel cut whole oat.

ॐ

PILAF (regular bulgur) A special type of cracked wheat which can be used as a substitute for rice.

ॐ

RICE (brown long grain) Can be cooked as a main dish. Rich in vitamins and minerals. Finest quality hulled by a special technique to fully preserve all the germ.

ॐ

RICE (brown short grain) Contains many vitamins and minerals. The short grain cooks into a fluffier and chewier grain.

ॐ

RICE (cracked) May be added to breads and muffins to increase the nutritional quality of the product. Serve as a cereal.

ॐ

RYE (whole) Dark northern rye for home grinding and cereals. This rye is offered in several grinds for everyday use.

ॐ

RYE (cracked) A staple grain found in northern Europe. This is free from flour. Use as a cereal or mixed with other meal. May be added to bread and muffins.

ॐ

RYE (rolled flakes) Use as an addition to baked products. Can be used as a cereal.

ॐ

SOYA GRITS (toasted) Lightly toasted soya beans cracked free from flour. Can be softened and added to soups and cereals to increase the nutritional quality of dishes.

ॐ

SOYA GRITS (raw) Soya beans cracked free from flour. Ready to eat except for softening. Grits may be soaked and added to cereals. May be added to soups or any dish as a meat extender.

ॐ

TRITICALE (whole) A cross between wheat and a rye grain. Larger than wheat, sweeter than most grains. Use in combination to experience a new taste treat. Delicately sweet. Add whole wheat flour to enhance the wheat flavor when using the grain in breads.

WHEAT BERRIES (high protein hard red spring) "Montana Spring Wheat" makes the best flour because of the quality of the high protein in the wheat.

WHEAT BERRIES (hard red winter) Use as whole berries, or ground, or for cracking.

WHEAT (cracked hard red) Cracked for use in breads and baked products. Use as a meat extender in soups or casseroles.

WHEAT FLAKES (red wheat) Use as a cereal. Use as a granola. Also use to increase the nutritional quality of baked products.

WHEAT GERM (raw) Germ used as a topping for desserts. Use to increase the nutritional quality of drinks.

WHEAT GERM (toasted) Germ toasted to insure a nutty-like flavor. Use as a topping and as an addition to drinks and breads. Especially nice in baked products such as muffins and cookies.

WHEAT GERM AND HONEY A combination of lightly toasted wheat germ and dehydrated honey. Delightfuly sweet, used in salads and drinks. May be used in baked products.

WHEAT GERM AND DATE SUGAR Lightly toasted germ. Date sugar added to the germ. Can be used as a topping for desserts, salads, and blended drinks.

CHAPTER 8

HERBS FOR
HEALTH AND HAPPINESS

The fundamental principle of true healing consists of a return to natural habits of living. Many people are in poor health because they do not have the *knowledge* necessary to maintain good health. Today, in this age of returning to the basic concepts of natural healing, many are finding cures growing naturally in their own environment. More and more people are becoming interested in learning about herbs and their use as remedies for diseases that afflict us.

There are many good books available on identifying herbs. Learning how to recognize and identify even one herb adds to your knowledge of survival concepts. Since the majority of herbs are perennial, you can find them in the same spots year after year. Some herbs are scorned as common pests and proliferate freely and vigorously in your own yard, needing no man's attention for their survival.

Growing your own herbs is great fun. They are strong plants and thrive with little attention. Some herbs are quite common and are easily found in your local supermarket. Garlic and onions are seldom sprayed with pesticides; they have their own built in pest conrol. Herbs not native to your region can be purchased in herb or health food stores. These herbs are dried and keep well in airtight containers.

If you gather your own herbs, you can easily dry them for future use. Always gather herbs at their peak. Some herbs bloom and should be gathered at that stage; others are so common that there is no need to store them. Gathering your own is fun, economical, and good exercise.

To dry herbs naturally, tie in small bunches and hang upside down to dry in a dark place where warm air circulates freely. After herbs dry, remove the leaves from stems by placing the whole stem in a paper bag and shucking the leaves off by hand. Store in airtight containers.

Since so many herbs are prepared as tea, it is important to learn how to make an excellent pot of same: Put your water on to boil. Scald tea pot and fill with hot water; this warms the tea pot. When the water is boiling briskly, empty the tea pot (recycle that hot water—don't pour it down the drain), put in herbs, and pour in boiling water. Replace lid on tea pot and wrap tea pot in a towel or cozy; allow to steep five to seven minutes, or until tea is the desired strength.

The following list of herbs are those we use and are familiar with. There are many more. Studying herbs is a lifetime occupation.

BASIL An annual herb commonly grown for kitchen use. It is used for seasoning tomato dishes, soups, spaghetti, vinegar, salads. Basil is good in almost anything! Basil leaf tea is a good sedative for jangled nerves. Basil has always been used for stomach problems and peps up a lagging appetite.

BAY LEAF (Bay Laurel) Another kitchen herb commonly used in soups and stews. If you put a couple of laurel leaves in your flour and grains, it will keep the bugs out.

BORAGE An easily grown annual. A good herb for convalescents. The fresh leaves make a nice addition to green salad; they taste like cucumber. Borage leaves and seeds stimulate the flow of milk in nursing mothers. The tea is a good blood cleanser. It is good for fevers, yellow jaundice, to expel poisons of all kinds due to snake bites, insect stings, good for coughs, and can be used as a gargle for sores in the mouth and throat.

CATNIP Catnip is a very old remedy. The tea can be given to children and infants. It is good for the relief of pain of any kind. It is good for gas, colic, fevers, worms, convulsions. Catnip will relieve headaches; it is soothing and quieting, a good remedy for nerves and feverish colds. If you are having a problem sleeping, make a tea with catnip and feel yourself drop off to slumberland. Catnip is a perennial plant and easily grown. It is a wonderful tonic for cats.

❧

CAMOMILE The flowers, fresh or dried, are the medicinal part of this herb. A good general tonic. Produces appetite and is good for weak stomachs. This herb is good when used to regulate monthly periods. Great for kidney, colds, bronchitis, bladder troubles, to expel worms, and for jaundice. The tea may be used to wash open sores and wounds. It is good for nervousness. May be used as a hair rinse and is especially good for light hair.

❧

CAYENNE Cayenne is a pure stimulant. It creates a sensation of warmth. Cayenne is good for coughs, chills, fever, gas. It is the best natural stimulant known to man. The habitual drinker considers it his best friend after a night of gaiety. He puts it in hot soup when sobering up. Useful in stomach cramps, fever, colds, and constipation. Cayenne may be taken in capsules. *Caution—excessive consumption of cayenne may cause gastroenteritis and kidney damage.*

❧

CELERY All parts of the celery plant can be used, even the root. Celery is always available in your local market. As a vegetable in salads, celery is beneficial for skin problems and provides necessary bulk for good elimination. It improves the appetite and promotes the onset of menstruation. Celery is a wonderful flavoring agent for soups and stews.

❧

COMFREY Good remedy for: coughs, inflammation of lungs, hemorrhage, tuberculosis, and asthma. The tea may be applied to bruises, sprains, swelling, and fractures, and will reduce swelling and relieve pain.

❧

EUCALYPTUS A native Australian tree now common in California. The leaves of eucalyptus trees are useful for repelling fleas. Pick fresh branches and tuck them under the mattresses, rugs, in your pets' bedding. The nuts have a wonderful odor and can be burned as incense in the fire place.

❧

GARLIC A perennial plant cultivated as a kitchen herb. Garlic stimulates the action of the digestive organs. It is also an expectorant, good for bronchial congestion. For coughs, take grated garlic with honey. Garlic is still worn as a necklace in many places today to ward off sickness and evil spirits. It's a must for spaghetti sauce and stew. Garlic is a good gopher repellant—plant it around your rose bushes.

❧

GINSENG Used in hot climates as a preventative against all diseases and illnesses. Promotes appetite and is useful in digestion. It is good for colds, coughs, and chest troubles. If it is taken when hot, it will produce perspiration. It is good for stomach and lung troubles; also good for problems of the urinary tract; and it aids constipation.

❧

GOLDEN SEAL This is one of the best blood purifiers known. Good for all stomach and liver problems. Good taken in small doses to aid pregnancy nausea. Bladder, sore gums, fever, smallpox; it will improve appetite and aid digestion.

❧

LAVENDER The fragrance of the leaves and flowers of this Mediterranean shrub are responsible for its popularity and cultivation in the United States and Europe. The tea is good for gas, headache, dizziness, nausea, and fainting. The dried flowers can be sprinkled among your linens for a delightful odor. Lavender is also good for warding off evil spirits. It was used in ancient times to perfume bath water.

❧

MALLOW WEED Mallow weed is considered by many people one of those pesky weeds to be gotten rid of, an impossible job. It grows freely in waste areas and gardens. It can only be used fresh, but this is no problem as it grows year round. For bronchial congestion, coughs, inflammation of the tonsils, make an infusion of mallow. Chop one to two teaspoons of this herb and let it stand in one half cup *cold* water for eight hours. Then heat to lukewarm and drink. (Do not boil or steep the herb in boiling hot water.)

❧

MINT A common garden herb cultivated for its refreshing taste. It is good as a tea or an addition to tea or fruit drinks. Mint teas can be taken for nerves, headaches, vomiting, and as an aid to digestion. Take only on occasion, as daily doses of mint tea over a long period are not good for your heart.

MUGWORT A perennial plant found along roadsides and fences all over the United States. This herb is also called sailors' tobacco and was used as a tobacco substitute at one time. When smoked it acts as a calmative when anxieties occur. Mugwort does not leave the head light as do most mixtures of smoking tobacco. Mugwort is legal; if you do not have local access to it, some herb shops stock it.

Mugwort is unsurpassed as a cure for poison oak. For small patches of poison oak rash, we make an infusion of mugwort and witch hazel:

Pack mugwort leaves into a pint jar with a tight fitting lid; pour witch hazel over to cover and let sit; it can sit this way for months; the liquid is then drained off and used as a lotion on the skin.

If you have to deal with a really super case of poison oak (we have), especially when the rash is near your eyes or mouth, here is an easy way to conquer it:

Use fresh or dried mugwort leaves; put a couple of handfuls of leaves in the bath tub and cover with hot water; let the herb steep in the hot water for five to seven minutes and then add enough cold water to make it bearable; now jump in the tub and soak in the mugwort; the wet leaves can be laid on your eyelids as you soak. Used in this way mugwort helps heal open wounds too.

If you are not familiar with this herb, it will be well worth your money to buy a herb-finder's book to help you locate it. This stuff works better than any commercially prepared medicine you can buy. Here in California, we find it grows right next to poison oak. As this plant dies down in the fall, it's a good idea to get a large supply of dried leaves in case of emergency. Here in the San Juan Canyon, it is at its peak during July and August.

This fascinating herb has also been used since ancient times to repel moths and other insects. Mugwort wards off evil spirits—a branch of it kept in the house is supposed to ward off the devil himself. John the Baptist is supposed to have worn a girdle of mugwort to help sustain him in the wilderness. If you are planning a hike, sprinkle mugwort in your boots—it wards off fatigue. Old legend has it that if you sleep on a pillow of mugwort, you are able to see your entire future in your dreams.

This herb is also good for female complaints when used in combination with marigold flowers. It is effective when taken as a tea to increase the flow of menstruation as well as relieving menstrual cramps in maidens. Mugwort has proven effective in relieving everything from a lonely heart to frustrations and anxieties.

Mugwort tea is useful for overcoming kidney stones and bladder infections. It is also useful for increasing the flow of urine. It has been known to relieve fevers and gout. Make a tea by steeping a tablespoonful of the herb in a pint of boiling water for twenty minutes. Drink a cup or two each day as needed.

❧

ONIONS Superb as a culinary herb, the onion also has valuable medicinal properties. Onion is supposed to strengthen the heart and lower blood pressure. It's good for gas pains and heartburn. It is a good expectorant. Onion juice mixed with honey is good for hoarseness and coughs.

When our children were growing up, we used this cough syrup to eliminate their coughing spells. After one dose of the syrup, the coughing nearly always stopped. The children used to say that just thinking about the syrup made them feel better.

Place 6 cut-up white onions in a double boiler. Add no water. Add ½ cup honey. Cook slowly over a low fire for a half hour. Strain the mixture. The mixture will stop a cough if you take it at regular intervals. The honey aids in building the blood stream, and the onion acts as a bowel cleanser. It is best to keep the mixture warm. If it is slightly heated, it will relieve the irritation as well as the coughing.

❧

OREGANO (wild marjoram) A perennial herb, always used in spaghetti sauce. Oregano is good for your nerves and has a beneficial effect on an upset stomach and indigestion. It helps relieve abdominal cramps and will help regulate the menstrual cycle when taken three or four days before the regular time.

❧

PARSLEY A commonly cultivated kitchen herb with wonderful flavor that is greatly appreciated by rabbits and humans alike! It is a beautiful garnish and good in salads. Parsley is a good expectorant and aids suppressed menstruation. Grow it as a border plant in your garden.

❧

PENNYROYAL Good for fevers. Will remedy toothache, gout, colds, chest, and lung problems, as well as cramps, headaches, sores in the mouth, pain. Helps with menstruation. Relieves nausea, but should not be taken by pregnant women. Good for nerves.

❧

ROSEHIPS A very good source of vitamin C. Gather hips in the fall, dry, store in dry place for winter tea. Good in jellies and syrups, too.

❧

SWEET MARJORAM This plant grows both as an annual and a perennial. It has a wonderful fragrance, and a tea made from it is good for gastritis and colic in children. An herb pillow stuffed with dried marjoram leaves is good for rheumatic pains and brings sweet dreams.

❧

WATERCRESS Cultivated for its leaves, which are used as salad greens or garnishes, watercress also makes good soup. It grows in clear cold water in creek beds, ditches, and streams everywhere. Watercress is recommended for gout and digestive disturbances. Its high vitamin C content makes it a good illness preventative. It is always used fresh. *Caution—do not use daily as excessive use can lead to kidney problems.*

HERBS USED FOR SPECIFIC DISEASES

Appetite Golden Seal, strawberry, marjoram, basil, ginseng, camomile.

Abcesses Carrot, slippery elm, grated raw potato.

Anemia Comfrey, dandelion, raspberry.

Asthma Comfrey, vervain, wild cherry, flax seed, horehound.

Bladder Juniper berries, comfrey, thyme, valerian, slippery elm, apple tree bark, mugwort.

Breasts (sore, swollen, caked) Comfrey, parsley, St. John's wort.

Bowel troubles Dandelion, catnip, slippery elm, vervain, tansy.

Cramps Cayenne, pennyroyal, fennel.

Coughs Comfrey, rosemary, ginseng, horehound, borage, garlic, onion, mallow.

Convulsions Catnip, peppermint, pennyroyal.

Chills Cayenne, peppermint, catnip, bayberry bark.

Colic Catnip, peppermint, pennyroyal, rosemary, golden seal, sweet marjoram.

Colds Peppermint, blue violet, catnip, ginger, garlic, pennyroyal, ginseng, elder, high mallow, onion.

Constipation Ginger, chickweed.

Enema Catnip, bayberry, strawberry, raspberry.

Fever Catnip, pennyroyal, apple tree bark, camomile.

Headaches Catnip, pennyroyal, camomile, yerba santana, thyme, elder, rosemary.

Kidney Cayenne, parsley, comfrey, spearmint, dandelion, camomile.

Laxative Golden seal, elder, horehound.

Loss of Speech Rosemary, red pepper, golden seal, wild cherry.

Liquor Hangover Scullcap, valerian. Make tea and give at one hour intervals, one-half ounce, until hangover subsides.

Nausea Ginger, mint, pennyroyal, spearmint, lavender.

CHAPTER 9

EDIBLE FLOWERS—
FUN AND FRIVOLITY

If you are one of those people who love to grow flowers, why not grow edible ones? They make an exciting garnish for many dishes, and if you have a great abundance, you can use them as a main course.

Nasturtiums, because of their peppery taste and beautiful color, make a dramatic display in a salad or floating in a bowl of clear soup. The leaves and seeds may be eaten as well as the blossoms. Nasturtiums are related to watercress. The seeds are a good substitute for capers. This hardy annual plant is easily grown from seed sown in the spring. Once you get them started, you'll have lots of volunteer plants from then on.

Violets have great beauty and flavor. The leaves and blossoms can be added to green salads. Imagine violets as a garnish on a bowl of granola! Pansies, which are related to violets, may be used the same way.

Take the time to candy some for desserts or cake decorations.

CANDIED VIOLETS

2 egg whites
1 cup white sugar

Wash and drain flowers. Pat gently between absorbent towels to dry thoroughly. Remove stems but leave flower petals intact.

Beat 2 egg whites until foamy but not stiff.

Sit down and relax.

Now dip each flower in the egg white or paint the egg white on with a clean soft brush to coat well. Place flower in dish of sugar, sprinkle flower with sugar, covering well on both sides. Now put the flower on waxed paper on a cooky sheet. Using a toothpick, shape petals and arrange flowers as they will be when dried. Be sure to keep flowers separated. Dry in the sun or a warm place. Store in an air tight container.

Other flowers may be candied. Borage blossoms and leaves and rose petals are beautiful prepared in this manner.

Calendula, also called garden marigold, is another easily grown annual that adds color and excitement to many meals. Try them in egg dishes. The blossoms may be used fresh or dried. Added to rice or pasta, they impart their beautiful golden color. Pull the petals from the fresh flower heads and dry on cookie sheets in warm place. Store in airtight containers for future use.

The old-fashioned day lily, *Hemerocallis aurantiaca,* a hardy perennial plant, produces many beautiful flowers each season. All are edible. You may use buds, open blossoms or end of the day blooms. They have a bean-like flavor and may be served as a vegetable. Day lilies are beautiful for Chinese wok cooking.

Squash blossoms are another fine edible, and if you are successful at growing squash, your plants always produce more than you can eat or give away. Pick the male blossoms for eating (the ones that have pollen). Remove centers. To keep blossoms from closing, wash in cold water and refrigerate until ready to cook. Try them dipped in fritter batter and fried quickly for breakfast!

Rose petals are edible and have a high vitamin C content. They should be separated from the stem and rinsed and dried gently.

The garden pink, dianthus, is also edible and tastes like cloves. The petals can be dried along with rose petals for teas and pot pourri.

If you are not growing your own flowers, make sure the ones you pick for eating have not been sprayed with toxic chemicals or fed with systemic plant food.

Sweet peas, forget me nots, chrysanthemums and lavender flowers are all edible. Let your imagination run wild!

Tea made from dried flowers is brewed like regular tea.

Caution—be sure all the flowers you eat are organically grown. Sprays and systemic plant care products are poisonous.

CHAPTER 10

MUSHROOMS AND NUTRITION

Modern science has done much to confirm the beliefs of many cultures regarding the fact that mushrooms have qualities of nutrition that set them apart from other foods. The results of many extensive research programs have established cultivated and wild mushrooms as an important nutritive part of our diets. The following represents a list of nutrients found in mushrooms.

PROTEIN Cultivated mushrooms are higher in protein than any vegetables. The protein contained in mushrooms is equal to the muscle protein.

VITAMINS Mushrooms provide a good supply of niacin and thiamine, as well as riboflavin, pyridoxine, folic acid, and vitamins C and K.

MINERALS There are small amounts of potassium, copper, iron, phosphorus, and calcium found in mushrooms.

LECITHIN This element is important to good health as it keeps cholesterol particles from building up in the arteries and other vital areas of the body.

AMINO ACIDS These are the building blocks of proteins that are essential to our diets. There are over twelve amino acids found in cultivated mushrooms.

CALORIES Mushrooms provide a perfect substitute for high calorie, fatty main dishes. There are 66 calories per pound of fresh mushrooms.

STORING

Mushrooms should be stored in the refrigerator where they can get plenty of air circulation. Always store mushrooms in paper bags; plastic wrap does not allow them to breathe.

PREPARATION

Wipe with a damp cloth and trim tips of the stems if they look like they need trimming. If you feel as if you must wash them, run a spray of cold water over them. *Never* soak them. Soaking destroys many valuable vitamins and minerals.

FREEZING

Although fresh cultivated mushrooms are almost always available, if you buy them at a bargain price you can freeze them for future use. Put the mushrooms in a rigid container with a tight lid. Do not wash them. They will keep a month frozen in this way. If you want to keep them longer than one month, blanch or sauté them lightly, put them in a container and freeze them. Use the blanched or sautéed mushrooms within four months.

BLANCHING

Some people like to blanch mushrooms slightly before adding them to other foods. This is an especially good procedure for the stronger tasting wild mushrooms. If you wish to blanch mushrooms, put the whole mushrooms in a pan with enough water to cover the bottom of the pan. Add a teaspoon of lemon juice to the water and a little sea salt. Cover and let them come to the boiling point. Simmer two minutes. We believe that the most nutritional way to eat mushrooms is raw. We add them to salads as well as main dishes. Mushrooms are nice served as an appetizer.

Try our recipe for MUSHROOM BURGERS: Sliced mushrooms combined with cheese and sprouts and grilled to make a sandwich is a healthful addition to any meal. Grill the cheese and mushrooms, add the sprouts once the cheese is melted. Cooking destroys many vitamins and minerals in foods as delicate as sprouts. We prefer to retain all of the nutritional quality in the foods we prepare.

Mushrooms are available fresh in our local markets year round. No need to worry about sprays or chemical additives because mushrooms can only be grown organically.

People have hunted wild mushrooms since the beginning of time. To those of you who are interested in learning to hunt wild mushrooms, a few words of warning: *MUSHROOM POISON IS DEADLY!* Even people who are considered experts in the field of mycology have been killed by eating poisonous mushrooms. Contact and join a local mycology club. Read books about mushrooms, the more the better, paying close attention to the chapters on poisoning and poisonous mushrooms. If you are not absolutely certain about the identification of the mushroom you have found—Don't eat it!

People who have a tendency to allergies must exercise more caution when eating wild mushrooms. First make sure of the identification of the mushrooms, don't mix varieties, eat only a small amount the first time to see if you have an allergic reaction.

You will find it helpful to keep a notebook on your mushroom hunting with sketches, spore prints, descriptions, taste, etc. Just learning the edible varieties in your own area may take years of study.

Hunting mushrooms is a fascinating hobby, good exercise, both physical and mental. We find plenty of edible varieties in our canyon environment. *Psalliota campestri,* the meadow mushroom, is plentiful in the rainy season. Always take more than one container on your hunt. Do not mix varieties in your containers. We always take a couple of baskets and a pocketful of paper bags. A pocket knife is very useful. There are times during the season when we pick many more mushrooms (especially the meadow variety) than we can eat. We wash and clean each one thoroughly, examining it closely to make sure of its identity and to be sure it is free from bugs and bruises. Using a large needle and string, we string each mushroom from the base of the stem through the top of the cap, cutting larger mushrooms in pieces. By hanging the mushrooms in the rafters above the parlor stove, we decorate our house and at the same time dry enough mushrooms for stews and spaghetti sauces for the next year. After the mushrooms are dry (hard and leathery) they are stored in clean canning jars with tight fitting lids. We put a couple of bay leaves in each jar to help preserve them well. These mushrooms can be soaked in hot water to reconstitute or simply crumbled and added to the spaghetti sauce and allowed to simmer with it until plump and juicy again.

Another common mushroom in this area is the puff ball. The smaller variety are about the size of golf balls here and snowy white against the fresh green of the meadow. Once in a great while we find a giant puff ball; these can be as large as basketballs! One, if it is white and firm clear through, is enough to feed an army. They are good sliced and dredged in flour, then sautéed until lightly browned in a skillet with butter. The puff ball goes from its white, firm, edible stage to a yellow-green gooey mess. If left alone this then dries and turns to a solid mass of dark brown spore. This dried puff ball spore is good for stopping the flow of blood from cuts.

The only tree mushroom in our area is the Chicken Mushroom, *Polyporus sulphureus,* easily identified by its bright almost psychedelic color. It is very good when it is young and tender, chopped and cooked with scrambled eggs.

These three varieties are good ones for any beginner to start with. Otherwise, play it safe and do your mushroom hunting in your local supermarket.

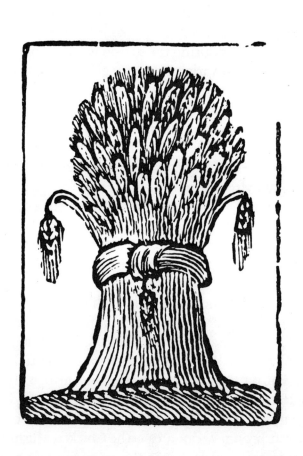

CHAPTER 11

BREAD AND BREAD MIXTURES

good loaf of bread is a basic necessity in the search for complete nutrition. The only way you can be assured that the very best ingredients go into your bread supply is to bake it yourself. Baking your own bread is fun, economical, and well worth the time it takes. Your family may be used to a steady supply of white, fluffy, "enriched" bread. We call it impoverished bread—it is "enriched" by the commercial baker with chemicals, and it lacks the balance of natural vitamins and minerals essential to a healthy body.

The bread you bake using the whole grain flours will be coarser in texture and heavier than store bought "double bubble." Two slices of your bread will be 100 percent more nutritious than a whole loaf of commercial bread. Take some time to explain this to your children; their bodies and minds will benefit from the knowledge.

Our own experience has proved that any hungry child will be better satisfied when he eats sandwiches made with homemade bread. Our children complained bitterly when we first began doing all our own bread baking. "But it's not sliced," they cried in alarm. So what? Everyone needs to learn something new once in awhile, another step toward self sufficiency. If you slice your own, you at least have a choice between thick and thin.

Making your own bread naturally makes you more aware of the waste of "leftover" bread—bread that is too dry or too small to make sandwiches of. *Don't throw it away.* We save every crumb! Bread crumbs make delicious cakes, puddings, and toppings for casseroles and desserts. If the bread is too hard to crumble by hand, chop it in your food grinder. Little squares of dry bread can be used as croutons in soups and salads and make excellent teething biscuits for cranky babies. Croutons are good stuffing material for baked turkey, chicken, or crown rib roast.

As long as your bread crumbs and croutons are thoroughly dry, they may be safely stored in suitable containers in your pantry. A suitable container in this case could be anything from a cookie jar to a paper bag!

There is definitely a knack to baking bread. Touch and feel as you prepare your bread dough and do not be afraid to add more or less flour than the recipe calls for.

GENERAL DIRECTIONS FOR BREAD MAKING

First: All utensils used in bread making should be scrupulously clean and scalded before using.

Second: Scald the liquid, add salt, sugar and fat; then cool to lukewarm temperature.

Third: Mix the yeast with ¼ cup lukewarm liquid, using yeast according to the time desired for the process. If the bread is to be allowed to rise overnight, use ¼ yeast cake to 1 pint liquid or ⅓ yeast cake to 1 quart liquid. For bread mixed and baked during the day, use 1 yeast cake to 1 pint liquid. If dry yeast is used, mix it with a little lukewarm liquid and flour several hours before adding to the sponge.

Fourth: Add the yeast mixture to the lukewarm liquid mixture.

Fifth: Sift the flour, allowing 3 to 4 cups for each cup of liquid. Add ½ the flour to the liquid mixture and beat thoroughly. Add more flour to make a dough, using a knife, until when touched with the finger, the dough does not stick to the finger. A bread mixer is a time and labor saver. Turn dough onto a slightly floured board; knead by pushing the dough into the palms of the hands and drawing it forward with the fingers. Use as little flour as possible on board and hands while kneading. Continue until the dough is smooth and elastic to the touch. It takes from fifteen to twenty minutes to knead with the hands and about three minutes in the bread mixer. Thorough kneading makes fine grained bread.

Sixth: Put dough in a bowl, cover closely, put in a warm (not hot) place and let rise to double its bulk. This may be overnight or in the daytime, depending on the quantity of yeast used. During the rising, ordinary room temperature, from 68 to 75 degrees F., should be kept. The length of time required for rising depends upon the room temperature; the process may be hastened by increasing the temperature from 75 to 88 degrees F.

Seventh: Knead again, shaping into loaves; divide dough into as many portions as there are cups of liquid in the mixture. Place in pans; if a dark crust is desired, brush over with skimmed milk or melted fat.

Eighth: Cover and let rise in a warm place to double their bulk.

Ninth: The baking is as important as the mixing of bread. The temperature of the oven depends somewhat upon the size of the loaves. If your stove does not contain an oven thermometer, test the oven by spreading one teaspoonful of flour one-quarter of an inch thick on the lid of a jelly glass and allow it to remain for 5 minutes in the oven. If the flour becomes golden brown, the temperature of the oven is between 400 and 425 degrees F.

Ten minutes after the baking begins, the heat should be decreased gradually. The time for baking bread is usually divided into quarters. The first quarter, the bread rises; the second quarter, it begins to brown; the third quarter, it finishes browning; the fourth quarter, the baking is completed and the bread shrinks from the pan. Bake loaves from fifty to sixty minutes.

Tenth: Cool loaves on a rack or place them so the air can circulate freely around the loaf.

TIPS ON BREADS AND HOW TO BAKE THEM

One cake of yeast or one package of dry yeast will raise eight cups of flour. If you are in a hurry, and need to bake the bread faster, you may use one package or cake of yeast to four cups of flour. With this method bread may be made in less than three hours. Cake yeast is perishable and must be kept in the refrigerator. The package dry yeast will keep for several weeks on a shelf. It will keep forever refrigerated.

Milk, water, or potato water may be used in baking breads. Each of them gives a different result. Water gives a crisper crust. Bread that is made from milk has more nutrition. Milk allows the bread to become browner and last longer. Potato water gives a coarser and larger loaf that will keep longer. Skim milk may be used in place of fresh whole milk. Powdered milk may be used to provide more nutrition and convenience.

Hard wheat makes the best dough. Hard wheat is not bleached or enriched. If you use white flour, it should always be sifted. Hard wheat has more protein and makes a more elastic dough. No more than one-sixth of the total amount of flour need be unbleached. If your recipe calls for six cups of flour, use five cups of whole wheat and one cup of unbleached.

Always sift the flour, then measure. Do not sift wheat flour.

Soy flour is made from the soy bean and is recommended in diabetic diets. It contains more protein and calcium and more B-complex than any other flour. Its protein is not in the form of gluten which makes the bread elastic and strong enough to rise. It is useful in increasing the food value of bread. Any amount up to one-fifth of the total flour used may be soy.

Buckwheat and rye are never refined although they may have preservatives added to them.

Cornmeal should be made of the whole corn kernel. Stone ground cornmeal has all the germ in it and can be found in most health food stores. The germ of the corn, as in any cereal grain, is high in oil, vitamin E, B-complex and protein.

Salt gives flavor and stabilizes fermentation.

Margarine, butter or lard can be used as shortening.

Eggs add flavor, color, and delicacy to the dough.

Wheat germ is the embryo of the wheat and is removed from enriched flour. Add two tablespoons germ to one cup white flour.

THE INTENSE LOAF WHEAT BREAD

4 cups milk
2 tablespoons salt
4 envelopes yeast (¹⁄₄ oz. each)
9 cups whole wheat flour
2 tablespoons oil
1 cup honey
²⁄₃ cup warm water
2 cups wheat germ
1 cup either: Wheat berries which have been cracked,
millet which has been soaked for three hours or overnight,
or rolled wheat. Any other crunchie dry grain is nice.

Heat the milk to near boiling. Stir in the honey, salt and oil. Cool to lukewarm. Dissolve yeast in warm water. Add 6 cups whole wheat flour to the milk and water and yeast mixture. Beat 300 strokes by hand. Add the remaining flour. Now add the crunchie dry ingredient of your choice. Add the wheat germ. Mix well, turn onto the board and knead. When you knead the dough, use as little flour on the board as necessary. We like to rub a little oil on the board. Knead until the dough becomes elastic. A good way to test for elasticity is when you press the dough in, it will bounce back at you. This is a sign the yeast is working. Let the dough rise in the oven if you have a pilot light in the oven. Pick a warm spot. Let it rise until it is doubled in size. Knead once again and shape into loaves. Grease pans and put the loaves into the pans. This rises until double in size. Bake at 350 degrees for forty-five minutes. Cool in pans. This loaf freezes well if you want to keep it any long period of time.

WHEAT BERRY BREAD OR ROLLS

2 cups warm water
1½ teaspoons dry yeast
½ cup gluten flour
¼ cup molasses
1¼ teaspoons salt
2½ cups cooked wheat berries
3 cups whole wheat flour
2 cups unbleached flour
¼ cup oil

Dissolve the yeast in the hot water. Substitute whole wheat flour if you do not have gluten flour. Add molasses, salt, berries, flours, and oil. This dough should be very thick and come away from the bowl. Turn the dough onto a floured board and knead with lots of flour until it does not stick anymore. Let the dough rise twice before baking in loaves or rolls at 375 degrees for one hour for bread. The rolls take less time.

SOY-SUNFLOWER BREAD

This recipe makes 2 loaves. Allow three and one-half to four hours time from start to finish.

1/4 cup warm water
1 tablespoon dry yeast
2 1/2 cups scalded milk (cool to 100 degrees)
6 tablespoons honey
1/4 cup oil (safflower, sesame or corn)
3 1/2 to 4 cups unbleached white flour

Sprinkle yeast on warm water in large bowl. Pour cooled milk, honey and oil over it. Add flour gradually until fairly smooth. Beat 100 strokes, whipping air into batter. Cover and let rise in a warm place thirty to forty minutes. This makes your sponge, which makes the mixing of the rest of the flours easier. It also allows the yeast to develop in the absence of salt.

2 tablespoons salt
1 1/2 cups soy bean flour
1/2 cup wheat germ
2 cups unbleached white flour
1/2 cup chopped sunflower seeds

To mix the above ingredients, shake together in a paper bag. Gradually fold into the risen sponge, using your hands as dough gets thicker.

Knead dough on flour board about five to eight minutes or until it "fights back."

Set to rise in greased bowl, covered, in warm place, until double in bulk. This will take about an hour.

Punch down, then shape into a solid mass and cut in half. Press out the air and form a loaf from each half. Place in greased baking tins. Let rise another twenty to thirty minutes in time.

Heat oven to 350 degrees.

Prepare *egg wash* (1 egg and 1/4 cup water, mixed well with fork). Just before placing loaves in oven, brush tops with egg wash, to make them shiny. If you wish, sprinkle poppy or sesame seeds on top.

Bake fifty to sixty minutes, until the bottom of a loaf sounds to hollow when tapped.

RAISED OVEN DOUGHNUTS

In a large sauce pan bring to the boiling point:

1½ cups milk

Remove from heat and stir in:

⅓ cup shortening
¼ cup honey
2 teaspoons cinnamon
2 teaspoons nutmeg

When lukewarm add:

2 large eggs, beaten
2 cakes of yeast (compressed or dry) softened in
¼ cup lukewarm water
4 cups flour

Beat dough until well mixed. Cover the pan and let stand in warm place until the dough is doubled in size, about one hour. Turn dough onto a well floured board and knead. Now you will have a soft ball. The dough will be soft. If batter seems too soft, add flour. Roll dough lightly, avoiding stretching, until it is about ½ inch thick. Cut into doughnuts with a cutter.

Place doughnuts 2 inches apart on a greased cookie sheet. Brush the doughnuts with melted butter and let rise in a warm place until they double in size. This will take about twenty minutes. Bake in a preheated oven 425 degrees for ten minutes. Be sure they are golden brown. As soon as the doughnuts are out of the oven, brush them with butter and sprinkle on cinnamon or nutmeg. This recipe will make about a dozen doughnuts.

MOLLETES—MEXICAN SWEET ROLLS

1 cup milk
2 tablespoons shortening
1 large egg, slightly beaten
2 tablespoons warm water
1½ teaspoons anise seed
½ cup honey
1 cake yeast
4¼ cups unbleached flour

To milk in sauce pan add anise seed and bring just to the boiling point. Remove from heat, add shortening, honey and salt. Mix well and let cool to lukewarm. Add egg and yeast. Mix well, making soft dough by adding flour. Cover with a damp cloth and let stand until double in size (1 hour). Turn onto floured board and divide dough into 24 equal pieces. Shape into balls and place 2 inches apart on a well greased baking sheet. Cover with a damp cloth. Allow to rise until double in bulk; this process takes about one hour, depending on the room temperature. Brush with a little melted butter. Bake at 350 degrees for twenty minutes. Yields one dozen medium sized rolls.

BRAIDED FRUIT LOAF

2 cups unbleached flour
2 cups whole wheat flour
1/2 cup milk
1/4 cup honey
3/4 teaspoon salt
3 tablespoons shortening
2 eggs, beaten
1/4 cup warm water
2 cakes yeast
2 teaspoons grated lemon rind
1 cup raisins
1 cup mixed dried fruits, chopped

Sift flour; scald milk in small saucepan, remove from heat. Stir in honey, salt and shortening. Cool to lukewarm. Measure water into two quart bowl and crumble in yeast. Stir until dissolved. Add lukewarm milk mixture and eggs and mix well. Add 1½ cups flour and beat until smooth, stir in lemon rind, raisins and fruit. Gradually add remaining flour. Turn out on floured board. Knead until smooth and springy. Wash and grease bowl and turn dough over to grease entire surface. Cover with towel and let rise in a warm place until double in bulk, about two hours. Cut into three equal parts. Roll each part into a rope 15 inches long. Place two ropes to form an X on a greased cookie sheet. Then place third rope directly over the X and braid, starting at center of the three ropes. Turn around and do the other side the same way. Cover with a towel and let rise until double. Bake thirty minutes in a 375 degree oven.

PANNETONE

3 cakes yeast
1 cup lukewarm water
1 cup unbleached flour
1/2 cup honey
3 cups stone ground flour
1 cup raisins
1/2 cup chopped walnuts
1 tablespoon anise seed
2 tablespoons honey
1 cup warm evaporated milk
1/2 cup melted butter
4 eggs, beaten
2 teaspoons salt
1/2 cup chopped almonds
1/4 cup chopped pine nuts
1 teaspoon vanilla

Dissolve yeast and 2 tablespoons honey in lukewarm water and milk. Add 2 cups flour, mix well. Add melted butter and honey and eggs. Add 4 cups flour to which the salt has been added. Cover, let rise in warm place until light. (About two hours). Add raisins, fruit, nuts, anise seed and vanilla. Add more flour, try to keep dough on the soft side. When smooth, put in bowl which has been greased. Cover and let rise until double. This takes several hours. Then shape into two large loaves. Let rise again in pans until double. Brush tops of loaves with beaten egg and 1 tablespoon water. Bake at 325 degrees for forty-five mintues.

HONEY CRACKED WHEAT BREAD

2²/₃ cup water
2 cups cracked wheat
¹/₂ cup honey
2 cakes yeast
2¹/₂ cups unbleached flour
3 cups whole wheat flour
¹/₂ cup margarine

Pour boiling water over the cracked wheat. Add honey and shortening and cool to lukewarm. Add yeast, flours and mix well. Knead. Let rise in greased bowl, punch down and let rise again. Punch down a third time and shape into loaves and place in greased baking pans. Bake at 350 degrees until golden. For a variety, you can make a wonderful cinnamon bread by adding cinnamon to the dough at the last rising. You may also add raisins, dates, apricots or anything you like. It will make a nice, sweet pannetone by adding fruit at the last rising.

HONEY SWEET BREAD

2 cups milk
2 cakes yeast
8 to 10 cups unbleached flour
1 cup margarine
¹/₂ cup honey

Scald milk and add margarine. Put into a large bowl. Let cool and add yeast and honey. Gradually add flour, enough to make a stiff dough. Knead until the dough becomes elastic. Let rise twice, once in the bowl and once in the pan. Bake at 350 degrees until done. Takes about forty-five mintues in most·ovens. This is a nice sweet dough that can be made into rolls or just used as a nice textured sandwich bread. Whole or broken bits of nutmeats kneaded into the dough, sprinkled with a little cinnamon or ginger makes a nice breakfast treat.

CHAPTER 12

NAN'S SOUR DOUGH COOKERY

Faced with the problem of trying to teach our children survival techniques, we decided to bake all our own bread. One day a week is set aside at our house as survival day. Bake the bread, chop the wood, and clean the house.

Sour dough has always been a favorite with us, and, realizing that it takes a lot of practice to make a good loaf of bread, we decided to concentrate on developing one good sour dough recipe that would produce a perfect and nutritious loaf.

The bread recipe calls for one quart of sour dough starter. We made our own starter, a simple process. Also there are many good commercially prepared sour dough starters on the market today. Since we like *sour* sour dough, we like to keep at least 6 cups of starter in the pot. The container you use to house your starter can be made of plastic, glass or pottery. Never put sour dough in a metal container. The acids in the sour dough can corrode the metal which then kills your starter, and it's definitely damaging to your health if you consume contaminated starter. We use a one gallon pickle crock. The lid of the starter pot should not fit air tight. Your starter is a living thing and needs the chance to breathe. As the yeast works in the pot, the starter may expand as much as double in bulk, so have lots of extra room.

SOUR DOUGH STARTER

To start your own sour dough starter, choose and clean your container well. Dissolve one package of Red Star dried yeast in 1½ cups of warm water. Stir in 2 cups of unbleached white flour. We are recommending Red Star yeast because it is the only dry yeast we have found in this area that does not contain chemical preservatives. Mix these ingredients together well and set your starter pot aside in a warm place (75 to 110 degrees) for about three days. At the end of three days or so the starter will be bubbly with a definite sour odor. In the San Francisco Bay area there is a wild yeast strain floating freely in the air which some people think is responsible for the wonderful tangy flavor of San Francisco sour dough. At this time (at the end of three days) you can increase your starter by adding equal parts of unbleached flour and warm water. *Never put anything in your starter except the unbleached flour and water from this point on.*

The older your starter gets, the more you use it, the better it is. If you use your starter frequently, you will want to leave it handy on the shelf in a place where the temperature is about 75 degrees. Stir it once in awhile and talk to it by all means. It will respond in a positive manner.

If you go away on a vacation, tuck it in the refrigerator and it will be fine upon your return. Starter can easily sit in the refrigerator a month without your attention. It can be completely revitalized by taking it out of the refrigerator twenty-four hours before you plan to use it, feed equal parts of flour and warm water and set in warm place.

If you have ignored your starter for a time, you will discover upon checking that the flour and liquid separate after a time, and the liquid is the color of good beer. The old miners drank this "hootch," which is certainly better for you than commercial beer—and every bit as intoxicating.

Twenty four hours before you plan to use your starter, feed it at least one cup unbleached flour and one cup warm water. This feeds the yeast and brings your starter to its full power.

Anyone who is a fanatic about housework and cleanliness is going to have a hard time adjusting to the behavior of sour dough starter. If the sides of your sour dough pot get crusty and sticky, it doesn't hurt the starter. If this condition bothers you, pour the starter out into another container and clean the pot using warm water and a scouring pad.

At this point let us add one of our favorite household tips. Sour dough starter makes an unbeatable paste!

This may sound elementary. You can increase or decrease the size of your starter by feeding or not feeding it. As long as you have one cup left over, you can always make more.

From this basic starter you can make the following recipes as well as many other exciting goodies.

SOUR DOUGH BREAD

Feed your sour dough starter at least one cup flour and one cup warm water twenty-four hours before you plan to start your bread. Put in a warm place (75 to 110 degrees).

1 quart sour dough starter
2 cups milk
2 tablespoons butter
¼ cup honey
1 package dry yeast
½ cup 7 grain cereal
½ cup wheat germ
3 cups whole wheat flour
   (you may substitute rye flour if you wish)
1 teaspoon salt
1 teaspoon baking soda
4 cups unbleached flour

Scald milk, add butter and honey. Pour into bread bowl to cool 'til lukewarm. This heats the bread bowl up. By the time the butter melts, the liquid is the right temperature to add the yeast. Add the yeast and stir to dissolve. Pour in the one quart of starter. Add 7-grain cereal, wheat germ, and 2 cups of whole wheat flour. Mix well. Blend soda and salt together in small bowl with fingers until smooth. Sprinkle over the top of bread batter and fold in gently. Cover bowl and let rise in warm place one hour.

We have an electric stove and we find the lowest warm temperature setting perfect for the rising process. We pre-warm the oven while we are scalding the milk and turn the oven off as we put the batter in to rise and place a pan of boiling water in the bottom of the oven (more about this later).

At the end of one hour, break down batter and stir in remaining unbleached flour until dough is too stiff to stir. Turn out on floured board and knead in the rest of the flour. The remaining one cup of whole wheat flour is used in this kneading process. Knead until dough is light and satiny to touch, about 500 times. Concentrate on putting your energy into the bread through the kneading process. If you get tired, cover the dough with a clean cloth and take a break. Better yet, put the kids to work helping you with this part of the bread making. Kneading is great therapy.

Place kneaded dough in a large greased bowl, turn dough over so the top is greased. Cover with a damp cloth and place in warm oven and let rise until double in bulk, about two hours. Place a pan of boiling water on the bottom of your oven. Take the pan out and reheat to boiling about every ½ hour. This helps keep the oven warm and adds needed humidity. This long rising process adds greatly to the sour dough flavor and texture.

Punch down dough. If the dough seems sticky, knead on lightly floured bread board. Allow to rest five minutes. Grease loaf pans well with oil or shortening and sprinkle bottom of loaf pans with sesame or poppy seeds. Shape dough into loaves, place in greased pans, turn to grease tops. Pans should be half full. Put loaves in warm place, cover with cloth and let rise one to two hours or until double in bulk. We put it back in the oven, repeating the process in the paragraph above.

When the bread has risen, uncover and turn oven on to 400 degrees. Leave the pan of boiling water in the bottom of your oven. Bake loaves at 400 degrees for twenty minutes, then reduce heat to 325 degrees and bake thirty to forty minutes, until bread shrinks from sides of pans and sounds hollow when thumped.

Turn out on rack to cool. Do not cover bread until it is completely cooled to room temperature.

We have experimented with containers for baking bread. The best container we have is a pottery bowl about 5 inches across and 3 inches high which was made for us by our potter friend. We wish for more bowls like this one. It makes an excellent crust. Until our wish comes true, we are using some stainless steel mixing bowls of about the same size; they hold 3½ cups of liquid. By using these smaller containers for baking, we get 5 or 6 loaves of bread. Everyone here loves the crust on the bread, and, of course, the smaller your loaves are, the more crust you have. This much bread lasts our family of five a week and sometimes we have a loaf left over. A loaf of sour dough makes a wonderful gift.

We store bread in the freezer. Let baked bread cool thoroughly on rack. Put in plastic bags, seal and freeze. You can allow the bread to thaw at room temperature or put in a brown paper bag, roll the edges of the bag up to seal and put in a 350-

degree oven for about one-half hour.

This bread slices easily and we always cut very thin slices. Toasted with butter and jam it is an unforgettable treat.

SOUR DOUGH PANCAKES

Feed starter 24 hours before. Mix together:

> *1 quart sour dough starter*
> *4 tablespoons cooking oil*
> *¼ cup wheat germ*
> *2 eggs*
> *½ cup evaporated milk or cream*

Stir well to mix thoroughly and then combine:

> *½ teaspoon salt*
> *1 tablespoon sugar*
> *¼ teaspoon baking soda*

Blend together with your fingers, eliminating lumps, sprinkle over the top of batter and fold in gently. Allowing batter to rest in warm place 30 minutes before using makes for better flavor.

Fry on hot, lightly greased griddle. The original sour dough pancakes were small, thin ones. The batter should be very thin.

If you are one of those people who hate to stand at the stove turning hot cakes while everyone else is eating and screaming for more, try this good method of serving the whole family at once:

Make the pancakes about the size of crepes, use an 8- or 9-inch cast iron skillet and make one at a time. Preheat oven to lowest warm setting and have a platter warming.

As your pancakes cook, place on platter in warm oven and drizzle some honey butter sauce on each one.

HONEY BUTTER SAUCE

¼ lb. butter
½ cup honey

Melt butter in pan, add honey, stir to mix and keep warm on back of stove.

SOUR DOUGH BISCUITS

1½ cups starter
1 cup milk
1 cup unbleached flour
½ cup wheat germ
1 cup whole wheat flour
1 tablespoon sugar
¾ teaspoon salt
1 teaspoon baking powder
½ teaspoon soda
salad oil or butter

Mix starter, milk, wheat germ, and whole wheat flour in large mixing bowl 12 hours before serving. Cover bowl and let sit in warm place to rise. If you are planning biscuits for dinner, do this much in the morning after breakfast.

Turn this very soft dough onto 1 cup flour on a bread board. Combine salt, sugar, baking powder, and soda with ½ cup of unbleached flour and sprinkle over the top. Mix dry ingredients into the soft dough by hand, kneading lightly to get the correct consistency. Do not overwork. Roll out to ½-inch thickness, cut out biscuits, dip in melted butter or salad oil. Place close together in pan. We use a cast iron skillet. Set in warm place to rise (thirty minutes to one hour). Bake at 375 degrees thirty to thirty-five minutes.

CHAPTER 13

YOGURT

Yogurt is almost the perfect food. It contains a high quality of proteins, minerals, and enzymes. It also contains all the known vitamins, including the ones that are hard to get, D and B-12. The action of the special bacteria that it contains, *Lactobacillus bulgaris,* makes it a pre-digested food. The body is able to digest yogurt twice as fast as ordinary milk. Yogurt destroys unfriendly bacteria in the large intestine and cultivates growth of friendly bacteria, "good flora." This bacteria helps to manufacture B vitamins and K vitamins. Yogurt prevents constipation. Yogurt is a natural antibiotic.

MAKING YOGURT

Take 1 cup of non-instant powdered milk, 2 tablespoons of fresh yogurt (from a natural food store), 3 cups of warm water or enough to fill a blender after all other ingredients are added. Blend all ingredients well; pour into container. Keep incubated for six hours or more. The incubation period will vary. The yogurt is done when it can be separated like custard. To use pasteurized milk, you must first heat the milk to just below boiling. Cool to lukewarm before adding the starter.

To make a homemade incubator, we use a box in which we put an electric heating pad on medium. You may also place the container in a pan of warm water and place it in the oven that is kept warm by a pilot light. Homemade incubation sometimes fails. There are many good yogurt incubators on the market.

Yogurt can be served with fruit. You may top the serving with wheat germ, coconut, bananas, honey, and any seeds or nuts that you like.

YOGURT SALAD DRESSING

1 cup yogurt
1 teaspoon honey
1/2 teaspoon paprika
1 tablespoon minced onion
1/2 teaspoon tarragon

Put into a blender, 1/2 cup of the yogurt with the remaining ingredients. Blend two minutes at high speed. Stir into remaining yogurt. Serves 4.

SUPER PROTEIN DRINK

2 cups of water
1 tablespoon honey
1/2 cup yogurt
6 ice cubes, cracked
1 tablespoon wheat germ
1 tablespoon vanilla
1 banana
1/4 cup any kind of fresh fruit
3 tablespoons protein powder

Mix together in the blender and drink. Unlike meat protein blender drinks, this tastes good. It is a super energy drink.

COLD YOGURT SOUP

1 cup chopped peeled cucumber
½ cup chopped scallions (white part only)
¼ cup chopped radishes (optional)
¼ cup dried currants
Salt to taste
Chopped fresh or dried mint
2 or more cups yogurt

Mix all ingredients in a bowl, using more or less yogurt for a thicker or thinner consistency. Delicious additions are a spoonful or two of cream and a clove of garlic put through a garlic press.

COON HEIGHTS SUPER PROTEIN DRINK

2 cups water
1 tablespoon vanilla
¼ cup strawberries
½ cup yogurt
1 tablespoon honey
1 banana
3 tablespoons soya powder
6 ice cubes, cracked

Blend all in the blender and enjoy.

TIGERS' AND PEOPLE'S MILK

¾ teaspoon lecithin powder
¼ cup nutritional yeast
1 tablespoon calcium lactate powder
1 orange, squeezed
1 teaspoon orange rind, grated
½ cup wheat germ
1 banana
1 teaspoon vanilla
¾ cup yogurt

Mix together in blender and drink.

CHAPTER 14

INTRODUCTION TO SOY BEANS

he soy bean is the most nutritious bean of all the legume family. It contains a good balance of all the elements our bodies need. Soy beans contain more fat than the average dry bean. They are rich in texture as well as protein and flavor. They are lower in carbohydrates than other dry beans. One advantage of eating soybeans is that they are alkaline, while many of the other beans people eat are acid. They are rich in lecithin and also contain all of the essential amino acids. The soy bean is the most valuable of all the plant foods because it supplies more nutritional value for the least amount of money.

In order to take advantage of soy beans, we like to cook extra in advance. We keep them in the refrigerator. Later we use them in soups, salads, loaves and patties. After reports on the bad effects of stilbestrol injections in beef, poultry, and other meats, we have decided that it makes more sense to introduce our families to recipes which contain soy beans. Soy beans have a hard shell. It is best to tenderize the shell before cooking the bean. We like to put the beans in an ice tray, cover them with water, and freeze them overnight. We run a little warm water over the tray and cook the beans along with the block of ice until the beans are tender; naturally the ice melts. Freezing the beans before cooking cuts down on the cooking time, saving energy.

SOY PASTE OR PULP

If the soy beans are to be used as a meat extender, do this: Drain them, as they must be free from moisture. Mash them while they are still hot, as they mash easier. This pulp may be refrigerated and used in patties, soups, loaves, or casseroles. Cold pulp makes a nice sandwich filling when a little green onion is added with a little chopped celery or parsley. We add a little mayonnaise so that it will spread smoothly. This same pulp also may be used as a dip for crackers or bread. It makes much more nutritional sense than most of the prepared dips. Use your imagination and create a nourishing as well as economical dish.

SOY BEAN SALAD

To one quart of cooked soy beans add one cup of onions sliced into rings, ¼ cup fresh parsley, ¼ cup chopped celery, 4 cloves chopped garlic, 2 parts oil to 1 part vinegar. Add one chopped tomato. Serve on a bed of lettuce leaves. Serves 4.

SOY BURGERS OR PATTIES

Add any vegetables to the cooled and mashed soy beans. Add salt and pepper to taste. Add any spice you enjoy. We like to alter this and all recipes according to our needs. If we are preparing Indian food, we add lots of curry. If we are preparing Spanish food, we add saffron. You may fry the patties or bake them. We sometimes add sesame seeds, carrots, celery, a little onion, a few raisins, and a bit of garlic. We have served them in place of meat patties when preparing meat for others. Soy burgers are good barbequed. We put the soy burgers on the grill for twenty mintues while we barbeque the red meat for others.

SOY BEAN LOAF

2 cups cold soy beans (cooked and mashed)
½ cup wheat germ
⅔ cup tomato sauce
1 cup bread crumbs
1 egg
salt and pepper to taste

After cooking the soy beans, mash them while they are hot. Combine them with remaining ingredients and form into a loaf and bake for forty-five mintues. You may alter this recipe by using potatoes or rice or chopped nuts in the loaf. Try the following recipe for buttered crumb topping for a final touch.

BUTTERED CRUMB TOPPING

Mix bread crumbs and softened butter together. Add:

herbs (whatever you like)
sea salt and pepper to taste
parmesan cheese if desired

Mix all ingredients together well and put on top of your soy bean loaf or casserole before baking.

SOY BEAN CASSEROLE

¼ cup diced salt pork
2 cups celery, chopped
2 tablespoons green pepper, chopped
6 tablespoons flour, unbleached
2 cups milk
1 tablespoon salt
2 cups cooked soy beans
1 cup buttered bread crumbs

Brown the salt pork in a fry pan. Add the celery and green pepper and sauté for about five minutes. You can use a little leftover meat or ham or omit the meat entirely. This depends on your individual style. Add the thickening made of flour, milk, and salt. Stir. Let this reach the boiling point and stir in the cooked beans. Pour the mixture into a greased baking dish and cover with buttered crumb topping. Bake in a 350-degree oven for thirty minutes or until the crumbs are browned.

SOY BEAN SOUFFLE

2 cups soy pulp
3 eggs, separated
2 tablespoons chopped parsley
sea salt and pepper to taste

Beat the yolks of the eggs and add them to the other ingredients. Fold well-beaten egg white into this mixture and pour into a baking dish. Bake at 325 degrees for thirty minutes or until it is set. Serve immediately.

TOFU (SOY BEAN CURD)—
THE MEAT WITHOUT A BONE

Tofu is made from soy beans and water. When you buy tofu, be sure to read the label to be certain that you are buying a brand that is free from preservatives. Tofu has the same nutritional value as the soy bean. Tofu can be added to soups, casseroles, and vegetable dishes, as well as scrambled with eggs and made into desserts. Tofu is a good source of protein and balanced amino acids. Our most recent invention, Jimmy Carter Pie…

JIMMY CARTER PIE

Blend together:

1 3 oz. package cream cheese
1/2 cup chunky peanut butter
1/2 cup honey
1/2 lb. tofu
1 pint of whipping cream

*Whip 1 pint of whipping cream and fold it into the peanut butter mixture. Pour into one cooked whole wheat pie shell (see pastry recipes). Refrigerate four hours before serving. We like to add four tablespoons of peanut butter to our pie crust mixture for this pie. The peanut butter can be added at the same time you add and blend the shortening to the flour in the whole wheat pie crust recipe. If you want, you may sprinkle a few peanuts on top of the pie to make it official.

BAKED TOFU LOAF

1 lb. tofu
½ cup bread crumbs
¼ cup chopped green onion
2 eggs
½ teaspoon grated ginger root
2 tablespoons tamari soy sauce
1 teaspoon sea salt
½ cup grated carrots
½ cup wheat germ

Squeeze water from tofu square. Combine all other ingredients. Place in a greased 8 × 8-inch baking dish. Sprinkle with ½ cup wheat germ. Bake at 375 degrees for forty minutes. Before serving, garnish with green onion (chopped). Serves 6.

TOFU BALLS

1 lb. tofu
2 large mushrooms, sliced
8 oz. crab meat
2 eggs
2 green onions, chopped fine

Squeeze water from tofu and mash fine. Add crab. Chop the sliced mushrooms fine along with the green onion. Add remaining ingredients and mix well. Shape into tiny balls. Deep fry in peanut oil. Serve with mustard and tamari sauce.

SCRAMBLED TOFU

1 lb. tofu
2 green onion stalks, chopped
2 tablespoons tamari sauce
⅓ cup shrimp
2 tablespoons oil
1 teaspoon honey

Drain all of the water from the tofu. Sauté along with the rest of the ingredients. Add seasonings if desired.

TOFU CHEESE CAKE

2 8 oz. pkgs. cream cheese
1 pound tofu, drained
1 teaspoon vanilla
¾ cup honey
2 eggs, beaten
⅛ teaspoon sea salt

Combine all ingredients. Blend with a fork until light and smooth. Pour into a spring form pan or a 9½-inch pie pan which has been lined with a crust, (see recipe below). Bake at 350 degrees for forty-five mintues to one hour. At the end of one hour, or when the cake is done, turn off the oven and allow the cake to sit without interruption for at least two hours. Place in refrigerator and do not disturb for at least six hours. We find the best results are obtained if the cake is made one day before serving. This allows plenty of time for preparation and aging.

CRUST

14 graham crackers
¼ cup melted butter
½ tablespoon honey

Crush crackers and mix well with butter and honey. Press into bottom and sides of pan before pouring in the filling.

ALTERNATE CRUST

¾ cups grated coconut
¼ lb. butter, melted
1 cup wheat germ
1 tablespoon honey

Melt butter. Blend all ingredients into butter. Line pan before pouring in the filling.

CHAPTER 15

THE CHAPTER ON CHICKEN SOUP

Many pages of writing about chicken soup may seem absurd to those who are used to recipes printed on file cards and pretty much cut and dried. This chicken soup thing is more than a recipe, it's a way of life for us. It has always been an institution with Jewish mothers. Chicken soup is good for everything from hurt feelings to the common cold.

There is nothing like a pot of homemade chicken soup simmering on the back burner. Once you understand the basic principles of chicken soup making, you will be able to use the knowledge you have gained to make a good pot of soup out of anything! If you think canned soup is good, you ain't tasted nothing yet.

When we were youngsters, we used to watch the cooks in our families put the juices from cooked vegetables in containers and place them carefully in the refrigerator. They explained to us that they kept these juices, as well as roasting juices from meats, for soup stock. This was perhaps our first lesson in ecology. It is possible to freeze these juices in the freezer. If you have a lot of juice, try freezing it in ice cube trays and storing it in the freezer in plastic bags.

Making a good chicken soup stock takes a couple of days, so always make a lot of basic soup stock and freeze what you don't need and/or send some to a sick neighbor.

For this excellent basic soup stock, you will need one whole chicken. It is also possible to use left-over chicken bones or you could buy a couple of chickens, use the boney pieces and giblets for stock, and do something special with the meaty pieces.

If you are fortunate enough to live in the country and raise your own chickens, don't overlook the fact that a home grown chicken is a far better end product than a commercially raised one. An old laying hen that is no longer producing enough eggs to justify her support makes an excellent pot of soup.

So now you have some leftover juices and the chicken and a big soup pot. Wash the meat and giblets, put them into the pot with juices and water—about a gallon of liquid or enough to cover the whole chicken for sure. Pour in about 2 teaspoons of sea salt and turn on the heat. Now cut the rooty bottom off of two yellow onions. You do not peel the onions as the skins give the broth a beautiful color. Cut the onions in half and add to the pot. You may wish to use some garlic as well: you do not have to peel this either (all of these vegetables are for flavor and color and will be discarded as the stock is strained). For sure you need celery: the celery leaves are excellent for flavor so if you are in the habit of throwing the celery tops away, don't do it! Add a few whole peppercorns or a small hot chili pepper, a turnip or two if you desire. Bring the stock to a boil and skim off as much of the foam that comes to the top as you can. Reduce the heat and simmer until chicken is tender. This much can be done the evening before you plan to serve the soup, and the soup pot can be left on the stove over a very low heat overnight.

Next morning, or when the chicken is tender, place a colander over a large pan and pour the simmered stock through the colander to strain. Refrigerate the broth and remove the chicken meat from the bones. You will problably want to chop some of the meat up to add to your soup. If you have a surplus, think about chicken salad for lunch.

Feed all of the skin and bones to your cats. Some of you may shriek at this, and that was our first reaction. We have always fed the skin and bones to our cats with no adverse effects: we feed them the flavoring vegetables as well. Along with some kibble or dog chow, they make a fine meal for the animals. The bones are soft after they are simmered well in the stock. If you are still squeamish about feeding bones to your animals, chop them up in the food grinder before mixing up your kitty's dinner! The roughage and marrow of bones makes them one of the most nutritious parts of the chicken. The skins supply your animals with some good old chicken fat, which is good for everything.

When the stock is chilled, you can easily skim all the chicken fat off the top and *save it!* You will need 4 tablespoons for your mocksa balls. The rest you can use for biscuits, greasing baking pans or whatever. It's a good hand lotion too.

Place the broth you will need back on the stove to heat. We usually allow about 8 cups for five people. Now is the time to freeze what is left over.

While the stock is heating, decide what vegetables you would like to use. Use your imagination and inventiveness on this part of the recipe. Some of our favorites are cabbage, green onions, leeks, celery, carrots, turnips—the list goes on and on. Wash and slice the vegetables thinly and set them aside with the chopped chicken. All of the vegetables should be crisp tender when the soup is served, so don't overcook. The meat is already cooked and only needs to be heated. The stock should not boil vigorously at this time; it should be simmered gently. You can add some dried herbs to the stock at this time if you desire. Two good ones are basil and summer savory.

Just as the soup is served, we sometimes add a garnish of chopped chives or nasturtium blossoms or calendula petals (see the chapter on edible flowers).

Now comes a very exciting part of this whole soup making experience. Papa developed this recipe because we are unable to find a local source for real matzo meal:

PAPA JOHN'S MOCKSA BALLS

¼ lb. cracker crumbs
    (saltine crackers come in a one pound box of
    four packages: use one package)
Scant 1 cup wheat germ
4 tablespoons chicken fat or butter
4 eggs, separated
2 tablespoons soup stock
herbs for extra flavor if desired
(basil, oregano or dried celery leaf)

Put crumbs, wheat germ, fat, lightly beaten egg yolks, and 2 tablespoons of stock in bowl. Mix well. Let sit five mintues, then add lightly-beaten egg whites. Put mixture into refrigerator to chill well.

Grease hands (use some chicken fat). Form mixture into small bite-sized balls, using one teaspoon for each ball. Cook in soup over medium heat until done.

If, as you read the above recipe, you wonder why the eggs have to be separated, the reason is that it makes better mocksa balls. The egg yolks are absorbed into the cracker crumbs and wheat germ, which makes for better flavor. The whites are added last to make the mocksa balls light and fluffy.

If you are worried about the part of the recipe that tells, or rather doesn't tell, about the cooking time—relax. Papa says the best way to do them is put the mocksa balls in the soup ten to fifteen minutes before you plan to serve it. He says it really doesn't make any difference how long you cook them—"Relax, good mocksa balls are good mocksa balls!" They are delicious left over, too.

Mocksa balls can be prepared ahead of time and allowed plenty of chilling time in the fridge.

The possibilities of chicken soup are endless; all you need is the good basic soup stock, and then you can let your imagination run wild. Homemade noodles are excellent in chicken soup. When you make raviolis, dry the leftover strips of dough in a warm oven and save for chicken soup, or use the recipe for ravioli dough to make plenty of noodles for many batches of soup. Rice, barley, wheat—all are good additions to chicken soup. By using your creativity, you can have a different soup every time. Using this basic pattern for soup stock, you could easily substitute turkey, pheasant, quail, or any fowl. If you are one of those people who throw the turkey carcas away after the Thanksgiving dinner, now is the time to change your ways. Put that carcass in the soup pot instead, and let your family reap the benefits. More marrow can be released into the stock by cracking the bones before they go into the soup pot. This is important if you are using only bones to make your basic stock. Use a hammer or cleaver to crack bones.

By learning to avoid waste in the kitchen, you can lower your food bills and have a much healthier diet.

COCONUT-MUSHROOM SOUP

1 large onion, chopped fine
3 tablespoons fresh parsley
1 cube butter
2 tablespoons flour
2 tablespoons curry powder
3 cups water
1 cup grated coconut
1 cup chopped mushrooms

Sauté onion and parsley in butter. Add flour and curry powder. Mix well, add water, coconut, mushrooms, simmer twenty to thirty minutes. Add 1½ cups of cream just before serving.

GAZPACHO (MEXICAN COLD SOUP)

1 onion, chopped
1 clove garlic
2 green peppers
2 cucumbers
pinch cumin
2 tablespoons paprika
⅓ cup olive oil
tomato juice
⅓ cup wine vinegar
dash tabasco

Puree all vegies in a blender. Add enough tomato juice to make a fairly thick soup. Add spices while pureeing some of the vegetables. Add oil gradually and blend after each addition. Add vinegar. Mix everything together very well and let stand at least overnight. Serve with garnishes; diced tomatoes, diced peppers, diced cucumbers; sprinkle the top of bowls with garnish. Serve with garlic bread or toast of your choice. This is a very special soup for summer meals when the time can be taken up with enjoying the garden or canning and sometimes even taking a late moonlight walk.

LENTIL SOUP

10 cups water
1½ cups lentils
2 stalks celery, chopped
½ cup chopped onion
2 or 3 sprigs of parsley
3 tablespoons oil
6 medium tomatoes, chopped
sea salt and pepper to taste
1 bay leaf
¼ teaspoon rosemary

Soak lentils three to four hours in the same water you will use to cook them in. Sauté celery, onion, and parsley in oil. Add sautéed ingredients to the lentils and water. Add tomatoes and seasonings. Simmer for three hours or until lentils are tender.

POTATO SOUP

2 cups potatoes, mashed
2 cups milk
1 tablespoon butter
¼ cup finely chopped onion
sea salt and pepper to taste

Steam potatoes until tender. Mash. Add milk, butter, and seasonings. Simmer over low heat until well heated.

TOMATO SOUP WITH CASHEWS

1 cup cashew nuts
1 teaspoon onion, chopped
3 tablespoons oil
dash basil
1 quart canned tomatoes
3 cups water
1 teaspoon salt
dash of oregano
1 tablespoon honey

Put all ingredients into a blender and blend. Heat it to a boil. Serve with sprouts and yogurt on top. This makes a very special soup.

PUMPKIN MUSHROOM SOUP

½ pound mushrooms, sliced
½ cup onion, chopped
2 tablespoons oil
2 tablespoons flour, unbleached
1 tablespoon curry powder
1 pound pumpkin, cooked and mashed
1 teaspoon nutmeg
sea salt and pepper to taste
1 tablespoon honey
1 cup milk

Sauté the mushrooms along with the onion in oil; add the flour and curry and stir. Add the other ingredients, all except the milk. Cook stirring ten to fifteen minutes. Add the milk; heat, but do not boil. Serve hot topped with yogurt if you like.

CUCUMBER SOUP

1½ large cucumbers, peeled & grated
2 cups water
1 teaspoon fresh chopped parsley
3 teaspoons onion
½ teaspoon sea salt
1 pint yogurt
2 springs mint
¼ of a fresh lime

Place the peeled and grated cucumbers in a heavy sauce pot and cover with water. Add the seasonings and herbs and cook for thirty minutes. Add two or three ice cubes and chill. Just before serving, beat in yogurt and mint. Add a few drops of lime. Very special on a hot day!

CHAPTER 16

SPROUTS

Sprouts are a quick and easy way to have fresh, vitamin-rich greens in the middle of winter. You can grow sprouts in a one-room flat, as they need no dirt for their development. Many seeds are suitable for sprouting and can be found in supermarkets or health food stores. Never go to a "feed and seed" place to buy seed for sprouting edibles. Some seeds have been sprayed with various chemicals and are poisonous to the body.

Aduki beans, kidney beans, oats, lima beans, wheat, alfalfa, soy beans…all make delicious sprouts. Sprouts are the ideal diet. It is said that the ideal diet can be cleansing and rebuilding, as well as maintenance for health, youth, and longevity.

SPROUTING INSTRUCTIONS

To begin with, find a warm spot to keep the sprouts while they are developing. Get a wide-mouth jar, the jar ring, and some wire mesh for the cover. It is best to begin sprouting with a seed that is easy to sprout. Alfalfa is a good one. Use one cup of seeds for a one gallon jar. Use three tablespoons of seed for a quart jar. Place the proper amount of seeds in the jar, cover with warm water, and soak them for eight hours. After this amount of time, rinse the seeds with warm water, drain them well, and put the jar on its side in a warm dark place (a cupboard is good). Rinse the seeds two or three times a day. The secret to success is to shake all the excess water off of them. As long as the seeds appear to be shiny, they are not dried out.

In three or four days, the sprouts will be about the same length as the seeds. Now you can put them into the sunlight so that they will produce chlorophyll.

They should remain in the daylight for several hours. Now the sprouts are ready to use in any dish. Sprouts will keep well in the refrigerator for several days. It is best to sprout in quantities that will be eaten in three or four days.

Sprouts are best served raw from a nutritonal standpoint and are good in salads, sandwiches, or mixed with other raw vegetables. Try sautéing them with fresh green onion and thinly sliced zucchini; at the last minute, scramble an egg into this.

SOME GOOD SEEDS FOR SPROUTING

ALFALFA Alfalfa sprouts are an excellent source of chlorophyll. They are rich in A, B complex, and C vitamins. They provide you with vitamins D, E, and K. The roots of field-grown alfalfa extend up to 100 feet into the earth and gather a wide range of minerals. The seeds sprouted indoors gather minerals from the water you rinse them in. Alfalfa is also a rich source of iron, calcium, and phosphorous. Alfalfa is used to rebuild decayed teeth.

LEGUMES (including peanuts) are especially hard to digest for most people because of a high concentrate of protein and starch and low moisture content. Sprouting them transforms them into a very high quality, easily digested nourishment.

MUNG BEANS The foods which are best suited physiologically are fruits and succulent greens. After three days of growth, mung bean sprouts become fruit in many ways. The protein becomes less concentrated and more digestible. The germination process converts starch to simple sugars. The carbohydrate content is the same as in casaba melon. The calorie content is slightly less than that of a papaya and a little more than a honeydew melon. Sprouted mung beans have the vitamin A value of a lemon, the thiamin of an avocado, the riboflavin of a dried apple, the niacin of a banana and the ascorbic acid (vitamin C) of a pineapple. Other legumes suitable for sprouting are lentils, green peas, chick peas, and soy beans. Try some of them and find your own favorites.

WHEAT Wheat is a staple food all over the world. When sprouted, wheat is a very acceptable food. Much of the starch in sprouted wheat is converted to simple sugars. The vitamin E content triples. Vitamin C is increased by a factor of six.

In the vitamin B complex, the individual vitamin increases range from 20 to 1200 percent. Like most whole foods, it is rich in laetrile (B-17), which selectively destroys cancer cells, but has little effect on normal cells. The laetrile content in sprouts and young fresh greens increases up to 100 times beyond that of the seed from which it originated. Sprouted wheat can be served in salads and many other dishes or even baked in bread. After being soaked in water overnight, the grain may be used as follows:

❧

CEREAL RECIPE 1 cup of wheat and 1 cup of wheat water, blended in the blender to desired consistency and sweetened to taste with dates or raisins.

❧

WHEAT MILK RECIPE 1 cup wheat and 2 cups water, blended in the blender and strained.

❧

BARLEY This seed was popular in the diet of the Chinese twenty centuries before the birth of Christ. It provides many nutrients.

❧

BUCKWHEAT Rich in rutin, which is necessary for maintaining a healthy bloodstream. Rutin builds up capillaries in the body, preventing hemorrhages. Buckwheat helps persons with high blood pressure and has a cleansing effect on the bloodstream. When used as a green, it has a high amount of lecithin.

INDOOR GREENS GROWN WITH SOIL

Indoor greens are grown on one inch of soil and are ready to eat in seven days. Obtain sproutable wheat, black unhulled buckwheat, or unhulled sunflower seed. Soak wheat fifteen hours and other small seeds eight hours. Fill a flat baking tray or any other flat pan with dark soil; we use fifty percent peat moss. Moisten the soil (no puddles). Spread the seeds next to each other and cover with wet paper and plastic sheet. Put in warm place. After three days, remove the cover. Place the tray in the light. Water as needed. After four additional days, they are ready to eat. This is a good source of economical sun vibrations year round.

❧

SUNFLOWER GREENS Soak unhulled seeds twelve hours. Fill tray with ⅝ inch of earth. Spread the seed on the soil and place 8 layers of wet newspapers and a plastic sheet on top. Take off pastic and paper when sprouts are 2½ inches high. Keep in sunlight until 6 inches high. Cut and eat.

SPROUT AND EGGPLANT ENCHILADAS

1 bunch green onions, chopped
½ teaspoon cumino
1 clove garlic
1 teaspoon basil
sea salt & pepper to taste
1 dozen corn tortillas
1 quart canned tomatoes, chopped
1 eggplant, chopped
½ cup alfalfa sprouts
1 pound cheddar cheese
½ cup wheat germ

Make a sauce by sautéing the chopped onion in oil with cumino, chopped garlic, basil, sea salt, and pepper. Add chopped tomatoes and simmer five mintues.

Chop the eggplant into small cubes. Chop the sprouts and add to the chopped eggplant. Grate the cheese.

Layer the ingredients in your casserole dish in this manner. Put some sauce on the bottom of the dish. Sprinkle wheat germ over the sauce. Next add a layer of eggplant and sprouts, then a layer of grated cheese and a tortilla. Build the casserole layer by layer, ending with a tortilla, the remaining sauce and grated cheese. This much of the work may be done ahead of time. Keep refrigerated until time to bake. Bake at 350 degrees for one hour and fifteen minutes.

CHAPTER 17

SALADS

A colorful salad can delight the eye and nourish the body. Salads are an important part of the noon and evening meals. There are many ways to combine fresh vegetables and fruits. Raw leafy vegetables are important to our nutritional intake. Fresh vegetables and fruits are rich in vitamins and minerals. Salads give us many precious elements.

It is a good practice to eat different types of salad each day. There are so many different kinds of vegetables available that there is no reason to become bored with the same type of salad at each meal. Try new combinations in order to alter the nutritional quality of your meals as well as taking advantage of the seasonal fruits and vegetables.

There are many tricks to salad making. One of our favorite tricks is to rub the inside of the salad bowl with garlic. This gives the salad a super garlic flavor.

Try developing your own combinations using the greens and vegetables as well as fruits available in your area. Try experimenting with various combinations. You will find your family members coming back for more!

JAPANESE BEAN SPROUT SALAD

2 tablespoons sesame seeds
2 tablespoons peanut oil
4 tablespoons honey
½ cup cider vinegar
½ teaspoon Tamari soy sauce
1 pound fresh bean sprouts

Heat sesame seeds in oil in heavy pan until seeds are lightly browned. Remove from heat. Mix with honey, vinegar and soy sauce. Let cool. Toss bean sprouts with the dressing. Serve at room temperature or refrigerate one hour.

LEMON SALAD

6 lemons
¼ teaspoon salt
¼ teaspoon pepper
1 teaspoon oregano
¼ cup oil

Peel and slice lemons. Add seasonings and oil. Let marinate one hour before serving.

TOSSED GREEN SALAD

1 head iceberg lettuce, cleaned and pulled apart
2 tomatoes (fresh), chopped
1 grèen pepper, sliced thinly
¼ bunch celery, cut up
1 head romaine lettuce, cleaned and pulled apart
2 green onions, sliced
1 raw beet, shredded
Oil and vinegar dressing

Combine all ingredients. Just before serving, add dressing and toss well.

ARTICHOKE SALAD

2 large artichokes, boiled
¼ teaspoon honey
½ teaspoon mustard
½ teaspoon sea salt
½ teaspoon paprika
2 tablespoons wine vinegar
2 tablespoons olive oil

Boil chokes until tender, remove from water and drain. Trim and peel off the outside leaves of the artichokes. Quarter artichoke hearts; place on bed of lettuce. Combine honey, seasonings, vinegar and olive oil. Pour over artichokes; serve.

LIMA BEAN SALAD

6 cups dried lima beans, cooked.
  Reserve 2/3 cup liquid.
1 clove garlic, minced
1/2 teaspoon sea salt
1 1/2 teaspoons honey
1/3 cup cider vinegar
1/2 teaspoon pepper
2/3 cup bean liquid
1/2 cup minced red onion
1/4 cup chopped parsley

Drain hot beans, save liquid. Mix garlic with remaining ingredients. Mix well with bean liquid.

WATERCRESS SALAD

1 bunch watercress, chopped
1 cup sprouts, chopped
4 cloves garlic, chopped
2 tablespoons oil
juice of 1 lemon
2 teaspoons cider vinegar
salt and pepper to taste

Mix cress, sprouts, and garlic. Pour seasonings, oil, lemon, and vinegar over greens and toss lightly. Watercress can be mixed into any green salad, or used as greens in sandwiches.

CHAPTER 18

SAUCES AND DRESSINGS

Sauces are a delicate part of cooking. Preparing sauces is the mark of a good cook. The right combination of ingredients will either enhance the flavor of the food or camouflage the true flavor of the food. A good sauce requires good ingredients. Sauces and dressings can be the springboard of many superb dishes and inspired meals. One can prepare many dressings and sauces ahead of time. The best ones are those that are made of simple combinations.

Simple salad dressings made from vinegar, oil, and honey seem to be best. Olive oil has been regarded as a basic food for years. Olive oil does not contain chemicals or preservatives. It will keep its original flavor and nutritional quality for a long period of time. Safflower oil is also used in dressings and has many vitamins and minerals. It is best to prepare sauces and dressings made from ingredients that add to the natural flavor rather than hide the original taste of the foods. Simplicity should be the key word when preparing sauces and dressings.

CHILI SALSA

8 medium-sized fresh tomatoes
3 hot fresh chili peppers
1 teaspoon cumin
1 teaspoon oregano (fresh is best)
2 cloves minced garlic
1 teaspoon salt

Wash and core tomatoes and chop fine. Remove stems from chili peppers and chop fine. Mix together with remaining ingredients and either refrigerate or put into canning jars to preserve for future use. The jars must be washed and sterilized and the salsa needs to come to a full boil before canning.

MEAT AND MUSHROOM SAUCE

1 small onion, sliced
1 clove garlic, minced
1/4 cup parsley, chopped
1/4 teaspoon pepper
1 1/2 cups sliced mushrooms
4 cups tomatoes, chopped
1/4 teaspoon nutmeg
2 teaspoons salt
4 teaspoons oil
1 pound ground beef
1 can tomato paste
juice of 1 lemon
1 teaspoon honey

Sauté onion, garlic, seasonings, and ground meat in oil until meat is done. Add rest of ingredients and simmer for three hours.

SQUID SAUCE

1 pound squid
3 tablespoons olive oil
1 small onion, chopped
1 can whole tomatoes (#3 size)
1 can tomato paste
2 cans water
juice of 1 lemon
salt and pepper to taste
1 teaspoon oregano

Clean squid, wash and cut into small pieces, dry on towels. Brown in oil along with onion. Add tomatoes, tomato paste, water, lemon, and seasonings. Cook two hours. Pour over cooked macaroni or any kind of pasta.

SHRIMP SAUCE

2 cups tomato sauce
1 large bermuda onion, chopped fine
3 tablespoons prepared horseradish
1 cup mayonnaise
½ teaspoon salt
1 tablespoon lemon juice
½ teaspoon cayenne pepper
½ teaspoon black pepper
2 cloves garlic, chopped fine

Mix all ingredients well. Keep in refrigerator until needed over cooked shrimp, crab or lobster.

OLIVE OIL DRESSING

1 cup olive oil marinated with
   2 cloves of chopped or mashed garlic for 3 hours
salt and pepper to taste
¼ teaspoon oregano
⅓ cup wine vinegar

Blend ingredients well just before using on salads.

VINEGAR AND OIL

¾ cup oil
¼ teaspoon oregano
¼ teaspoon pepper
½ cup vinegar
¼ teaspoon salt

Mix all ingredients well.

LEMON DRESSING

1 cup olive oil
dash of basil
juice of 4 lemons
salt and pepper to taste
dash of oregano

Blend all ingredients well. Good on any green salad.

HERB DRESSING

1 clove garlic, minced
¾ cup olive oil
½ teaspoon pepper
4 tablespoons basil
4 tablespoons oregano
½ teaspoon salt
8 tablespoons vinegar

Mix well in quart jar. Good on salads.

GARLIC DRESSING

2 teaspoons dry mustard
1 cup wine vinegar
9 cloves garlic, minced
2 cups oil
1 teaspoon salt
2 teaspoons oregano

Mix all ingredients well. Store in quart jar in refrigerator. Good for all green salads.

ITALIAN SALAD DRESSING

8 tablespoons olive oil
1 clove garlic, minced
1 teaspoon salt
2 tablespoons wine vinegar
juice of 1 lemon
1 teaspoon fresh ground black pepper

Place oil in bowl, add garlic and stir. Add remaining ingredients and mix well.

CHAPTER 19

MEAT AND MAIN DISHES

If you have a good butcher, you will probably have access to good meat. If you trade with a butcher who buys organically grown meat, you will experience a feeling of relief knowing that the meats have not been injected with chemicals and preservatives. All meat is not safe to eat. Today most cattle are injected in the feed lots. The best way to assure yourselves of chemically free meat is to raise your own or buy from a reliable source. Sometimes it is possible to purchase organically raised beef from friends who raise their own meat.

It is best not to plan all meals around meat. There was a time when a meal would not be complete without meat as the main dish. Today it is not practical to eat lots of meat. Meat is expensive. It makes more sense to plan meals around main dishes which include fresh vegetables, grains, legumes, seeds, nuts, eggs, and cheese. There are many foods which far surpass the nutritional quality of meat. Many of the lesser meats such as organ meats, ox tails, and stewing meat are better choices economically as well as nutritionally.

The following recipes were designed with nutritional quality, economy, and taste in mind.

FILET OF SOLE SAUTE AMANDINE

6 filets of sole
1/3 cup butter
3 tablespoons blanched, slivered almonds

Sauté the filets of sole over a gentle flame in the butter. When the filets are delicately brown, transfer them to a heated serving platter and keep them hot. Raise the flame under the pan, and in the remaining butter, quickly fry the almonds until golden brown. Pour the hot butter and almonds over the filets of sole and garnish the dish with lemon quarters and fresh parsley. Serves 6.

FRIED RABBIT

1 frying rabbit, cut up
1 onion, chopped
4 tablespoons oil
4 sprigs fresh parsley
salt and pepper to taste
1/4 teaspoon oregano
1/4 teaspoon rosemary
1 bay leaf
1 6 oz. can tomato paste
3 cups water

Sauté rabbit and onion in oil for ten minutes. Add seasonings, tomato paste, and water. Bring to a boil, simmer for one hour or until meat is tender.

LIVER SPREAD

2 slices fried liver
2 eggs, hard boiled
2 small red onions
¼ teaspoon sweet basil
¼ teaspoon salt
¼ teaspoon cayenne pepper

Put liver, eggs, and onions through food chopper. Add seasonings and spread on french bread.

ENCHILADAS CON QUESO

Sauce:

1 tablespoon safflower oil
1 medium sized onion, chopped
¼ cup chopped green pepper
3 cups tomato sauce or puree
2 tablespoons chili powder
salt to taste
1 teaspoon cumin
1 cup water, added gradually

Filling:

1½ pounds grated Monterey Jack cheese
1 large onion, chopped
1 cup ripe olives, pitted and chopped
2 dozen corn or flour tortillas

To make the sauce, fry the onion and green pepper lightly in oil. Add tomato sauce or puree; add the chili powder, salt, and cumin. Cook for ten minutes or until blended. Add water to thin sauce if needed. Thicken with a little whole wheat flour if necessary. To put the enchiladas together, dip the tortillas in the sauce one at a time. Now place them in a large pan and put a little cheese and some onion along with some olives on the tortilla and roll it up. Now bring the sauce to a boil and pour it over the enchiladas. Sprinkle some cheese on top and bake at 350 degrees for forty minutes.

BROCCOLI CASSEROLE

1 bunch fresh broccoli, steamed and chopped
1/2 cup mayonnaise
1/2 cup sharp cheddar cheese, grated
1/2 cup white sauce (made from milk, butter, salt
    pepper and a little flour for thickening)
2 cloves of garlic (crushed in the sauce)
1 egg, beaten
1 cup bread crumbs or wheat germ

Mix all ingredients in a 9 × 5 × 13-inch pan. We drain the broccoli and layer it with the rest of the ingredients. Top with bread crumbs or wheat germ; bake at 350 degrees until bubbly, about forty minutes.

ZUCCHINI CASSEROLE

3 cups cooked brown rice
4 cups cooked and mashed zucchini
1/2 cup grated onion
1/3 cup fresh chopped parsley
1/3 cup olive oil or butter
1 cup sharp grated cheddar cheese
1 clove garlic, minced
1/2 teaspoon sweet basil
dash of rosemary
salt and pepper to taste
3 eggs, slightly beaten

Mix all ingredients together and place in greased casserole. Bake at 350 degrees for thirty minutes.

SPROUT BURGERS

Add gradually in blender:

2 cups of sprouts
2 eggs
green onion, chopped
1/3 cup milk
2 tablespoons oil or butter
1/2 teaspoon salt
1/2 teaspoon pepper

Tuna or other cooked fish may be added if you want. After blending, mix in about ¾ cup flour. The mixture should be the consistency of pancake batter. Pour onto a hot grill or pan. The pan needs a little oil. Instead of blending the sprouts, you can add them after the other ingredients have been blended if you desire.

SPINACH FRITTATA

1 cup of spinach, sautéed
6 well-beaten eggs
1 onion, chopped
1 tomato, chopped
1 clove garlic, diced or minced
1 teaspoon kelp
1 teaspoon oregano
¼ cup wheat germ

Sauté spinach or kale in a little oil and garlic. Sauté until the greens are soft and tender. Beat eggs well and add remaining ingredients, including greens. Pour into a 6-inch fry pan. Cook until done in the center. Turn from time to time in order to cook evenly. Serve with a little yogurt, perhaps a few sprouts, on the side. Makes a nice brunch. If you are using meat, you may sauté bacon or any sausage of your choice along with the greens and add them all to the beaten eggs before cooking.

SOY BEAN CASSEROLE

2 tablespoons chopped onion
2 tablespoons green pepper
2 cups celery, chopped
6 tablespoons flour
1 teaspoon salt
2 cups milk
2 cups cooked soy beans
1 cup buttered bread crumbs

Brown the onion, pepper, and celery. Add thickening made from flour and milk. Cook until it all reaches boiling. Stir in cooked beans and pour into buttered casserole. Cover with bread crumbs and bake at 350 degrees for thirty minutes, or until the crumbs are brown.

RAVIOLI

Spinach filling:

> *1 cup spinach, chopped and cooked until tender*
> *1 cup Ricotta cheese*
> *1 egg, beaten*
> *salt and pepper to taste*
> *3 tablespoons grated Parmesan cheese*
> *1 tablespoon bread crumbs*

Drain spinach well in colander and press until dry; mix with Ricotta, egg, seasoning, Parmesan, and bread crumbs. Note: If the spinach filling is too moist, add more bread crumbs.

Prepare dough as follows:

> *1½ cups unbleached flour*
> *1 cup whole wheat flour*
> *2 eggs, slightly beaten*
> *⅛ teaspoon salt*
> *3 tablespoons cold water*

Heap flour onto bread board and form a well in the center. Drop in eggs, salt, and water and work with a fork to make a stiff dough. Knead lightly. Roll dough out very thin on a lightly floured board in a rectangular shape. Let rest five minutes. Spread filling over one half of the dough, fold other half of dough over filling to cover. Place a ravioli rolling pin on the dough and roll slowly; this shapes the ravioli. Use a ravioli cutter to separate the ravioli. (A pizza cutter does not work, as it does not seal the edges of the dough). At this point you may freeze the ravioli for future use by placing on cookie sheets, freezing and then storing in the freezer in plastic bags.

Cook ravioli in boiling salted water about ten minutes. Serve with butter sauce or tomato sauce generously sprinkled with Parmesan cheese. Serves 6.

This same dough recipe makes excellent noodles. Just make the dough, roll out, let rest five minutes, cut in strips of desired width and dry in a warm place. If they are dried well, they may be stored in jars with tight fitting lids right on your cupboard shelf.

GARLIC SPAGHETTI

1/2 cup olive oil
2 cloves garlic, sliced thin
1/2 cup parsley, fresh chopped
4 quarts water
1 tablespoon salt
8 oz. spaghetti
grated dry Romano or Parmesan cheese

Sauté garlic and parsley in oil until garlic is tender. Do this over low heat so as not to burn the garlic and parsley. After a few minutes, remove from heat.

Heat water to boiling point. Add spaghetti and salt. Boil spaghetti ten to fifteen minutes until tender but firm. Drain in colander. Place drained spaghetti on a large platter, top with the hot oil sauce and cheese.

CHAPTER 20

CEREALS, QUICK BREADS, AND PIES

omemade cereals are far better than the pre-packaged products found in most supermarkets. Homemade cereals are less expensive to prepare and more nutritious! Cereals can be served at any meal. Sometimes a light meal of homemade cereal and toast is a welcomed change.

Here are two of our favorites:

FAMILIA

Dry cereal with fruit:

> *3 cups quick oats*
> *3 cups wheat flakes*
> *1½ cups wheat germ*
> *2 cups raisins*
> *8 oz. dried apricots, chopped*
> *1 cup raw sugar or turbinado sugar*

Mix all ingredients together and store in refrigerator. You may replace any of the dried fruit with another dried fruit of your choice.

CRUNCHY GRANOLA

5 cups regular rolled oats
1 cup wheat germ
1 cup grated cocount
½ cup sunflower seeds (hulled, unsalted)
1 handful raw cashews or raw almonds
½ cup sesame seeds
salt to taste

Place this mixture in a large roasting pan. Mix together 1 cup oil, ½ cup honey, and 1 tablespoon milk; heat until warm and well mixed together and pour over granola. Mix well. Place in 275-degree oven and toast until golden-brown, stirring occasionally. Add raisins or any other dried fruit if desired. Serve with milk and add dates, bananas, or other fresh fruit in season for additional nourishment.

Quick breads are a welcome addition to meals. They are easy to prepare and require no advance preparation. Quick breads are generally a welcome after-school treat. You can take many standard quick bread recipes and add and alter ingredients to suit the need for more nutritional quality. Sometimes a little wheat germ or a little whole grain added to a simple quick bread recipe will enhance the quality and texture of the bread.

LOVING PANCAKES

Beat 3 eggs.
Slowly add ¼ cup unbleached flour, beating constantly. Stir in ¼ teaspoon salt, ½ cup milk, and 2 tablespoons melted butter. Grease a 10-inch iron skillet. Pour batter into cold skillet. Slip into oven heated to 400 degrees. Bake fifteen minutes at 400 degrees, ten minutes at 350 degrees.

Serve with topping of your choice. Honey Butter Sauce is a good one. Look in our sour dough chapter for this sauce. Yogurt and fruit mixed together also make a refreshing and nutritious topping.

WHEAT GERM PANCAKES

2 cups flour (one whole wheat and one unbleached)
1 egg
½ cup wheat germ
2 tablespoons baking powder
¼ cup oil
1 tablespoon honey
1 teaspoon salt

Mix all ingredients together to make a thin batter. For variety, we like to slice in a banana or add a little orange juice along with some grated orange rind. Bake on grill until golden on each side. Serve with a little honey and yogurt over the top.

FRED'S VINEGAR PANCAKES

½ cup flour (whole wheat)
½ cup wheat germ

To the one cup of dry ingredients add:

1 pinch of salt
2 teaspoons baking powder

Royal brand baking powder is the most natural we know of. It is made from grapes.

In a separate bowl, pour one cup of milk. Drop two eggs into the milk along with 1 tablespoon vegetable oil, 1 tablespoon honey, and 2 teaspoons of cider vinegar. Add this to the dry ingredients. Mix only enough to moisten. Do not over-mix, as the results will be terribly heavy pancakes.

ZUCCHINI PANCAKES

2 cups uncooked zucchini, grated
1/2 cup flour
1 teaspoon baking powder
salt and pepper to taste
1 egg, well-beaten
oil or butter for frying

Put zucchini into a bowl; add flour and baking powder. Now add salt, pepper, one egg and mix. Fry in an oiled or buttered pan as you would pancakes. Makes about 12 pancakes. Good hot as well as cold. Excellent served with yogurt as a main dish or as a side dish.

BAKING POWDER BISCUITS

1 cup unbleached flour
1 cup whole wheat flour
4 teaspoons baking powder
1 teaspoon salt
2 tablespoons shortening
3/4 cup milk

Mix dry ingredients. Work in shortening with fingers. Add milk gradually and put on a floured board. Pat and roll lightly to 1/2-inch thickness. Shape with cutter and bake in hot oven (450 degrees) for twelve to fifteen minutes.

HOT PARMESAN BREAD

1 loaf bread (preferably hot from the oven)
1/4 cup oil
1/4 cup dry grated Parmesan or Romano cheese
1 teaspoon oregano

Slice the loaf of bread in half lengthwise. Spread oil over each half. Now sprinkle rest of ingredients over the oil. This may be toasted slightly in the oven or served immediately.

WHOLE WHEAT TORTILLAS

2 cups whole wheat flour
½ cup unbleached flour
½ teaspoon sea salt
¾ to 1 cup water

Blend the flour and salt. Stir enough water in to make a stiff dough. Knead on a floured surface until it is smooth and elastic. Break the dough into 1-inch rounds and roll into very thin tortillas. Cook over low heat on a lightly greased griddle or fry pan, turning them one or more times. This recipe makes 18 to 20 tortillas, depending on the size.

SUNFLOWER LOAF

1 cup grated carrots
1 cup sunflower seeds
1 cup wheat germ
1 cup tomato juice
2 tablespoons butter
4 eggs, slightly beaten
salt and pepper to taste

Mix all of the ingredients and form into a loaf. Place in oiled baking dish. Bake one hour and fifteen minutes in a 350-degree oven. Serve with yogurt and a salad.

CINNAMON BREAD OR ROLLS

1 cup butter
½ cup honey
6 eggs (you may work with one or no eggs,
  depending on what you have; six is rich)
2 cups unbleached flour
1 teaspoon baking powder
1 cup chopped walnuts

Cream butter and honey. Add the eggs one at a time, beating well after each addition. Sift the flour and baking powder together. Mix ¼ cup of the flour into the nuts. Fold the remaining flour into the creamed mixture. Now fold in the floured nuts, pour into a well-buttered 8-inch loaf pan. Sprinkle the top with chopped walnuts. Bake at 350 degrees for fifty minutes.

LEMON NUT BREAD

1 egg
2 to 3 teaspoons fresh lemon peel, grated
½ cup water
1 cup honey
¾ cup milk
¼ cup oil
½ teaspoon salt
2½ cups whole wheat flour
1 teaspoon baking powder
1 cup chopped nuts

Combine egg with lemon peel and beat well. Combine egg mixture with the remaining liquid ingredients and beat well. Add the liquid all at once to the dry ingredients; stir just until moistened. Put into a loaf pan. Bake at 375 degrees for forty minutes to one hour. Cool before cutting.

APPLE BREAD

¾ cup honey
1 cup bland vegetable oil
3 eggs, slightly beaten
2 teaspoons vanilla
½ teaspoon salt
1 teaspoon ground ginger
2 teaspoons cinnamon
2 cups apples, grated
½ cup raisins
3 cups whole wheat flour
2 tablespoons baking powder
½ cup wheat germ
1 cup chopped nuts

Mix and blend honey, oil, and eggs. Add vanilla, salt, and spices. Add apples and raisins. Then dry ingredients, including nuts. Bake in a loaf pan at 350 degrees for one hour and fifteen minutes or until done. Cool before slicing.

CORN BREAD

1 cup unbleached flour
1 cup stone ground corn meal
½ cup whole wheat flour
2 tablespoons baking powder
2 tablespoons rice polish
⅓ cup wheat germ
1 teaspoon salt
2 eggs beaten or 2 tablespoons lecithin
2 cups milk or buttermilk
½ cup oil
1 tablespoon honey

Mix all ingredients together and bake at 350 degrees for twenty-five minutes. Bake in an 8 × 8 × 2-inch pan.

EGG BISCUITS

4 cups unbleached flour
1 cup wheat germ
3 tablespoons baking powder
2 tablespoons shortening
2 well-beaten eggs
2 teaspoons honey
1 teaspoon salt
1 cup milk

Mix quickly into stiff dough. Roll out lightly on floured board to ½-inch thickness, then cut biscuits to size and bake in hot oven (400 degrees) fifteen to twenty minutes.

WHOLE WHEAT AND BRAN MUFFINS

1½ cups milk
¾ cup honey
1 egg
1 cup whole wheat flour
1 cup bran flakes
2 tablespoons baking powder
½ cup oil

Combine milk, honey, and egg. Gradually add flour, bran, and baking powder. Add oil; beat well enough to mix. Spoon into greased muffin tins. Bake at 350 degrees for twenty minutes or until golden. Raisins, nuts, or any spice may be added.

In preparing pies, it is best to use the best quality ingredients available. Our latest invention, Jimmy Carter Pie, is filled with nutritious ingredients. The pie is one of the few ways that many people will eat tofu. The nutritional quality of this pie is unsurpassed. Look for it in our chapter on soy beans! Try it out on your own family and have fun with the following recipes.

WHOLE WHEAT PIE CRUST

⅔ cup oil
1 cup whole wheat flour
¾ teaspoon sea salt
4 teaspoons cold water

Mix with hands or fork the oil, flour, and salt. Mix until the mixture is like Parmesan cheese. Now add the water and blend into a soft dough. Add more flour if the dough is too soft; more water if the dough becomes too hard. The mixture should stick together. Roll out on floured board. Makes one 9-inch pie crust.

FLAKY PIE CRUST

2 cups unbleached flour
1/2 cup whole wheat flour
1 cube butter
1 teaspoon sea salt
1/4 cup cold water

Blend flours with butter. Blend to the consistency of Parmesan cheese. Add salt and water. Mix until smooth. Let rest in bowl for ten minutes. Allowing the dough to rest makes for a finer quality crust. Roll out on a board which has been floured with whole wheat flour. Bake at 350 degrees according to the type of pie or pastry you are making. Some pies require a raw shell that is baked with a filling. Some pies require a cooked shell that has been baked ahead of time. Makes two 9-inch pie crusts.

PEANUT PIE

1 cup or more raw peanuts
3 eggs
1/2 cup honey
1/8 teaspoon sea salt
1 teaspon vanilla
1/4 cup melted butter
1 cup corn syrup
1 unbaked pie shell

Place peanuts in bottom of unbaked pie shell. Beat eggs well. Add honey, salt, vanilla, corn syrup, and butter to beaten eggs. Pour over peanuts. Bake at 350 degrees for forty to fifty minutes. Serve hot or cold with or without whipped cream on top.

APPLE PIE

8 cups peeled and sliced apples
1/2 teaspoon nutmeg
3/4 cup honey
1/2 cup whole wheat flour
1 unbaked pie shell
1/4 cup lemon juice
2 tablespoons butter

Mix the apples, nutmeg, honey, and flour and place in unbaked shell. Pour lemon juice over the top. Dot with butter and cover with pie crust. Bake at 400 degrees for one hour. Make a hole in the middle of the crust so the steam can escape.

STRAWBERRY PIE

1 quart berries, cleaned and hulled
3 tablespoons arrowroot
2/3 cup honey
1/2 cup boiling water
1 baked 8 inch pie shell
1/2 cup whipped cream, sweetened

Sort berries, reserving the larger ones. Mash and mix the smaller berries to make one cup. Blend in arrowroot, honey, and crushed berries in a small saucepan. Add boiling water and cook, stirring constantly until thickened and clear. Cool. Place whole berries in baked pie shell and pour the cooked strawberry mixture over them. Chill and serve with the whipped cream.

PERSIMMON-APPLE PIE

2 cups persimmon pulp
1 cup milk
1 teaspoon cinnamon
1/2 cup chopped nuts
1 teaspoon vanilla
2 cups grated apple
1 teaspoon nutmeg
1 egg, well-beaten
1/2 teaspoon salt
1/2 cup raisins
1 unbaked pie shell

Mix all ingredients and pour into an unbaked pie shell. Bake at 350 degrees for forty minutes. Pie is done when knife is inserted and comes out clean. When pie is cool, let set in the oven after the oven has been turned off. You may serve with whipped cream.

WHEAT GERM CAROB CHIP PIE

1/2 cup butter
1/2 cup honey
1 cup wheat germ
2 eggs
1 cup carob chips
1 1/2 teaspoons vanilla
1 unbaked 9-inch pastry shell

Melt butter and cool. Gradually beat in honey. Add wheat germ, eggs, carob chips, and vanilla. Beat with a spoon about two minutes or until creamy and blended. Turn into pastry shell. Bake in 350-degree oven forty to forty-five minutes or until knife inserted in center comes out clean. Top with whipped cream.

CHAPTER 21

PASTRIES AND DESSERTS

Desserts and pastries can be a healthful complement to a nutritious meal. When you use the best quality ingredients, you can be assured that even your desserts and pastries will be filled with vitamins and minerals. A taste treat such as poppy seed cake is a delicacy never to be forgotten. Desserts can be filled with vitamins and minerals according to the quality of the ingredients used.

ITALIAN BISCOTTINI

6 tablespoons melted shortening
2 cups honey
6 eggs, beaten
2 teaspoons anise flavoring
2 cups unbleached flour
1 cup whole wheat flour
4 teaspoons baking powder

Mix melted shortening and honey together. Add beaten eggs and anise. Gradually add flours and baking powder. Mix well. Dough should be the consistency of cake batter. Grease pan and line with wax paper for easy removal. Pour in dough. Bake at 350 degrees until done. Remove from pan. Slice in the center and then into slices. Place under broiler and brown lightly on both sides. Yummy for dunkin'.

POPPY SEED CAKE

1½ cups poppy seeds
6 eggs, separated
½ cup honey
1 cup vegetable oil
2 teaspoons vanilla
1½ cups dry bread crumbs
2 teaspoons baking powder
1 cup whole wheat flour

Cook poppy seeds in a pan with enough water to cover them. Simmer them for twenty minutes, then drain and cool. Separate eggs; beat the yolks until lemon-colored. Gradually add honey, oil, vanilla, and poppy seeds. Add the bread crumbs and blend well. Add flour and baking powder. Beat egg whites until stiff. Now fold egg white into cake batter, folding only enough to mix together well. Put into tube pan, greased, and bake one hour at 350 degrees. Cool before cutting. Super!

SESAME POWER FUDGE

2 cup honey
1 cup peanut butter
1 cup carob powder
1 cup sunflower seeds
½ cup coconut, grated
½ cup raisins or other dried fruit
1 cup sesame seeds

Heat the honey and peanut butter. Quickly add carob powder and then all the rest of ingredients. Pour into square pan and refrigerate to harden. Cut into squares. Try to keep this refrigerated if possible.

HEALTHY CANDY

½ pound dates
1 pound dried apricots
1 pound dried figs
2 cups cut-up nut meats
½ cup raisins
1 teaspoon sunflower seeds
1 teaspoon grated orange rind
1 teaspoon grated coconut

Put all ingredients through food grinder with the exception of the seeds, rind, and coconut. Mix well. Press into buttered dish and cut into squares. Roll in rind and seeds or coconut.

CAROB MOUSSE

1 cup carob chips
4 eggs, separated
whipped cream (optional)
grated carob (optional)
½ teaspoon vanilla

Beat yolks lightly. Melt the carob over low heat, then add vanilla. Stir into the yolks. Beat egg whites until very stiff and fold into the cooled chocolate mixture. Turn into small dessert cups or dishes. Decorate with a thin layer of whipped cream and grated carob on top. Serves 6.

CARROT CAKE

2 eggs, beaten
1/2 cup oil
2 1/2 cups whole wheat flour
2 cups grated raw carrots
1 1/2 teaspoons salt
2 teaspoons vanilla
1 cup chopped nuts
2 cups grated coconut
1 #2 can crushed pineapple

Mix all ingredients well. Bake at 350 degrees in a 9 × 13-inch oblong pan which has been greased. When out of the oven, prick holes on top of the cake with a tooth pick. Make the holes close together.

TOPPING FOR CAKE

1/4 cup buttermilk
1 teaspoon vanilla
1/2 cup honey
1/2 cup butter

Mix together. Heat over medium heat until all ingredients are melted and blended. Cool. Pour over cake.

APPLE CAKE

2 eggs
¾ cup honey
½ cup oil
2 teaspoons vanilla
2 cups unbleached flour
2 teaspoons baking soda
2 teaspoons cinnamon
dash of sea salt
4 cups raw apples
1 cup chopped nuts
½ cup wheat germ

Mix eggs, honey, oil, and vanilla. Sift in flour, soda, cinnamon, and salt. Dice apples; add these with the nuts. Add wheat germ. Bake in a 350-degree oven in a 9 × 3-inch pan. This batter will be stiff and messy…enjoy working with it.

CREAM CHEESE AND HONEY FROSTING

3 tablespoons butter
6 oz. cream cheese
1 dash vanilla
½ cup powdered sugar
    (this is the balance that our head needs, not our bodies)
enough honey to blend into a nice spread

Mix all ingredients. Frost cake. Allow to sit for at least one or two hours before serving.

KUKU BADEMJUM (EGGPLANT CAKE)

2 medium large eggplants

Seasonings:

> *1 teaspoon sea salt*
> *¼ teaspoon freshly ground pepper*
> *¼ teaspoon turmeric*
> *½ cup chopped walnuts*
> *4 eggs*
> *6 tablespoons butter*

Bake eggplants at 375 degrees until tender when pierced with a fork, about thirty-five minutes. When cool, peel them and mash the pulp. Mix in seasonings and walnuts. Add eggs, mixing thoroughly. Melt butter in a heavy skillet. Spread eggplant mixture in skillet, flattening top; bake at 350 degrees for thirty minutes or until it holds together as a cake. Cut into pie-shaped wedges. Serve hot or at room temperature.

The eggplant cake keeps well in the refrigerator for two to three days. When serving, let it come again to room temperature or reheat in a little butter.

PERSIMMON CAKE

2 cups persimmon pulp
2 cups raisins
2 teaspoons oil
2 cups chopped walnuts
1 cup honey

Mix all well and combine with:

3 cups flour
½ teaspoon cloves
1 teaspoon sea salt
2 teaspoons cinnamon
2 teaspoons baking powder

Mix all ingredients with about 1 cup milk. Bake at 325 degrees for one hour.

CAROB-SUNFLOWER SEED COOKIES

1/2 cup honey
1 egg
1 cup oil
1 teaspoon vanilla
1 1/2 cups unbleached flour
3 tablespoons carob powder
1 teaspoon baking powder
1/2 cup sunflower seeds
1 tablespoon liquid (any juice or milk)

Cream together honey, egg, oil, and vanilla. Add rest of ingredients. Make dough that may be dropped onto sheet. Bake at 350 degrees for ten minutes or until lightly brown.

SESAME CRUNCHIES

1/2 cup oil
1/2 cup honey
2 eggs
1 teaspoon vanilla
1 cup oats
2 1/2 cups whole wheat flour
1/2 teaspoon sea salt
2 teaspoons baking powder
1/2 cup sesame seeds
enough liquid or juice to make soft dough

Cream oil, honey, eggs, vanilla, and add dry ingredients. You may add any juice you like in order to form soft dough. Drop onto cookie sheet and bake at 350 degrees for ten minutes or until golden. For variety, you may add different nuts and chopped dried fruit of your choice.

HONEY APPLE COOKIES

1 cup shortening
2 cups honey
2 eggs
2 cups unbleached flour
4 cups whole wheat flour
1 cup dried apples, cut up
3 teaspoons baking powder
1½ teaspoons cinnamon
1 teaspoon nutmeg
1½ cups raisins
2 teaspoons vanilla

Cream shortening, honey, eggs, vanilla, and add dry ingredients to make a dough that can be rolled out. Bake at 350 degrees for fifteen minutes. Cut into bars.

CRUNCHY SESAME SQUARES

4 cups oatmeal
1 cup sesame seeds
1 cup coconut, grated
½ cup wheat germ
½ cup walnuts, chopped
2 cups oil
6 eggs
2 cups whole wheat flour
2 cups honey
2 teaspoons vanilla

Mix all ingredients and put into a flat pan with sides about 1½ inches high. Bake at 350 degrees until golden and cut into squares.

CHAPTER 22

DEVELOPING THE BALANCE

For many who have not seen the possibility of survival, the lessons in survival may slip by unnoticed. In order that we may teach the message of survival, we must first of all be prepared to work on our own individual survival twenty-four hours a day. The message that we deliver through the format of this book is a message of the ways and means we have found effective for our own families.

The message could be summed up in one word. The word we use to demonstrate our personal survival system is *moderation*. Moderation means balancing the body and mind in order to maintain control of our own lives. Many times we are influenced by the people and places in our environment. Each day presents many stimulating choices. As we work to maintain the balance, we are often left only with a feeling of anxiety and frustration. Many times our choices do not complement our desire to maintain personal balance.

We have many tools available to us. These tools help us maintain our balance. The food we take into our bodies is a very important tool. We should learn to control and use food as one of the tools that will help us maintain our body and mind balance. It does no good to eat "organic" potato chips and pay good money for "health food" products when we can learn to grow our own food and harvest our own crops, which will provide our families with the freshest, most nutritional foods available. In order to survive each day we must learn the basic concepts of survival. We must hear the words of survival systems that might save our lives as a family of people living on the planet. We must be willing to risk everything ordinary. In the risk, we may gain one extraordinary benefit.

It is not always possible to balance the body and mind in keeping with the balance of the planet. The environment becomes a total distraction, because most of us allow the distractions. We give value to many distractions in the environment. We do special exercises as a daily habit in order to maintain our balance. As we practice moderation, we feel the effects of our methods and techniques. As the stresses and strains of our daily living cause stress throughout our minds and bodies, we learn to release these stresses. We use our survival concepts as tools of survival. It is best to develop a system of survival that is practical for our individual environment.

Many years ago we learned that our families would not accept a radical change in our diet. We introduced our families to a simple style of living. We all need time to alter our style according to our individual needs. While attempting to eliminate most of the prepared foods in our daily lifestyle, we tried to replace the food with an appealing alternative. The results of our experiments have been proof that the methods and techniques brought health and happiness to our families.

As we prepare our traditional meals, we eliminate most of the processed food items and replace them with natural ingredients that are filled with vitamins and minerals. When we discovered that sugar drained our bodies of vitamins and minerals, we replaced most of the sugar in our recipes with honey. Today it is easy for us to tell people not to use sugar. The price of sugar has gone up. It is less expensive to use honey. It is easy for us to advise people to cut down on their meat when the price of meat has gone sky high. Today many people are confronted with the high price of coffee. Coffee is a luxury in our homes. When we enjoy a small cup of coffee, we consider it a special event. The price of a box of prepared cereal has made bulk cereals and grains appealing to the general public. It makes sense for us to evaluate the price of preparing meals made from boxed and bagged prepared food items. The economical and nutritional reasoning behind preparing meals from real live foods has created a new way of life for many people. Many people are beginning to understand the basic concepts of eating balanced meals made from the best quality ingredients available.

Today moderation has become a way of life for many people. We can no more eat a diet of sugar coated wheat flakes than we can eat a diet of organic papayas. We must all learn to establish a balance in our nutritional intake and we must learn to establish aims that are within the realm of our daily lives—it is up to the individual to examine and re-evaluate his nutritional and psychological needs.

Sooner or later, we each must develop our own way in order that we might survive on a planet that is slowly losing energy. It has become obvious that the planet's natural resources are being used up at a steady pace. As we prepare ourselves for a changing future, we must be aware of the changes that must occur in our daily survival plan. Many survival methods have worked in the past, and some of them are still working. It is never too late to change our methods and adapt ways that make more sense for the times.

A special part of our day is enjoying the food we take into our bodies. The way in which our bodies react to the foods is the proof that the body is utilizing all of the vitamins and minerals we take into our system. There does not have to be any question as to how the body reacts to nutritional intake. When the body rejects some food, we might consider paying more attention to the quality of foods we eat. If your body develops dysentery every time you eat fried bananas, you may have to alter your diet. The body gives off many signs and messages. The proof of this message is how your body feels to you. If you feel good, it is possible that you are consuming the required amount of nutrients for your body.

Each body is different and reacts differently. The right balance and moderation form a regimen that will suit your *individual* environment. If you care about your body and mind, you must rely on the fact that it's possible your independent survival is dependent on your control and your ability to control and practice moderation at all cost. Once we understand how our individual control works, we stop acting like robots and begin a life of bliss. After a little practice, self control becomes a family word. We don't have to eat everything that is put in front of us. It is possible to live an independent life filled with health and happiness.

With the acceptance of our individual environment, a balance will present itself. In order to re-examine our present day lifestyle, we must examine the possiblity of changing that style to fit the needs of the environment as it stands today. It is difficult to develop our own individual way when there are many choices in the environment that influence our individuality. Many times the "other side of the fence" appears to be more inviting than where we are, in terms of our ability to develop our own methods of individual survival. Survival means feeling good from within. When we are able to work effectively and feel good about ourselves, our individual survival methods are working for us...the balance is moderation!

CHAPTER 23

PLANNING AHEAD FOR SURVIVAL

CONSERVATION

Water is the most basic element we need for survival. You can live for weeks without food, but only two or three days without water. Water is the most precious fluid we have. In the event of an emergency, the public water system or supply may be contaminated. We should depend on our own source of water. You should have available to you one gallon of good drinking water per person per day. This does not include water for showers or washing, things which are not considered essential during emergencies. We should all keep in mind how essential it is to keep more water handy if you live in a dry area. If you live in a remote area, you may get by with less water if you have a deep well. Most of us should prepare at least one gallon of drinking water per person for two or three weeks. Do it now...

There are many ways to store water: some people use tanks; others use five gallon cans. The least expensive way we know is to collect gallon milk bottles. Wash them out with soap and hot water, rinse well with a little chlorine and fill them with fresh water. Add a few drops of chlorine to the water. Cap the bottles and store them away for an emergency. Store the bottles in any nook and cranny in the house. A few drops of chlorine will keep the water sweet for years. Do not use bleach as it does not dissipate; chlorine does. Bleach is a combination of chemicals which may be harmful to the body if taken internally. Chlorine dissipates when

119

exposed to the air. If you can your own food, a good way to store water is to fill the jars as they are emptied with water and store them. By this method, the jars are used all year round and are functional, not just taking up space on the shelves. If you want, you can hot pack these containers filled with water and the canning process will eliminate any bacteria. If you do choose to can these jars, do not add any chlorine to the jars.

Wine bottles are good for storing water. They can be filled with water and a few drops of chlorine added. The bottles can be corked for future use. The tops of cabinets and refrigerators are good places to store spare bottles which have emergency water in them. Large wine bottles add a nice touch to a kitchen as well as being a practical place to store precious water for use in the event of an emergency. On cold mornings when the pipes are frozen, the bottles of stored water have been a relief when we need water to drink and cook with.

When you are working to provide the family home with water, you should consider the water system an important factor. It makes more sense to develop a water system that operates on a gravity flow basis than to rely on electricity. If you have ever experienced living in a house with no outside power, you realize how important it is to conserve the resources available. When you have to carry water to your home for drinking as well as bathing and cooking, you soon develop a respect for energy-saving devices such as piped-in water.

It would do each family good to reserve one day and one night a month for living without outside power. Each member of the family can experience living without outside power. In the event of an emergency, the family unit can be prepared to survive with the emergency supplies and energy available. The people who have learned to deal with the problems of not having outside power are more able to deal with conservation.

Survival concepts will not come easy to people who have had no exposure to living without outside power. But we *can* adjust to living a new way with the available resources—with each adjustment we become more confident. We begin to trust our ability to survive in a sensible, civilized manner, in a world that is ever changing.

As we see it, *preparation* is the key word in our survival plan. Many people have not developed the habit of preparing or making long range plans. Unless some preparation is made around the real necessities, life will become tiresome. Without the basic necessities, many will not live. As we see it, *food, shelter, love and lots of* hope are the survival tools of the future. Without all four tools, life and living can be very difficult. Living each day and developing a sense of control over our lives becomes the number one factor in our survival plan. Unless we learn to prepare now, there can be no future…

We do not feel it is wise to worry about where the water will come from in an emergency. We feel it is wise to make preparations for that emergency *now*. We have found many ways to conserve water around the house. Making sure that all of the faucets have good washers on them helps to preserve water. Drippy faucets are the cause of many gallons of water loss per year. Each family member needs to develop his own system of water conservation. We need to take responsibility for our own conservation system. We have found that developing a system of taking showers and baths can save gallons of water per day. There are devices sold in hardware stores that cut down the amount of water which comes out of the pipes.

TOILET TRICKS

One of the tricks is to put a brick in the toilet tank. Through the years we have eliminated flushing the toilet after each urination. Although the problems of water conservation have become obvious, this habit offends many people, but we continue to take no responsibility for those who are offended by our efforts to conserve precious water. We have developed the habit of observing others. We feel it is important to *our* own survival to speak out for survival techniques in general whenever it becomes necessary, because we realize that the only way people are going to change their daily habits of living is if they see that change is necessary.

We can change the patterns of our individual families. Taking care of the system of brushing our teeth and using water to do it can save many gallons of water during the course of one day. Many of us can use a cup instead of letting the water pour out of the faucet. We can change our methods of washing and watering. We can design new systems that will conserve the available resources and make life easier for all of us. We accept the fact that some seasons are dry and some are wet. While we observe many people carrying banners that read, *think rain,* we see others reverting back to their old habits of not thinking about conservation. All of the rain dances are not going to seduce the spirits to produce rain unless people conserve their resources on a twenty-four hour a day level.

Water is a purifier. Water washes out the toxins stored in the body. Water relaxes the body. One of the simplest pleasures of life is to feel hot water on our bodies. There have been months when there was no hot water or cold water coming out of the pipes in our homes; there have been many nights when taking a tub or shower bath was impossible. It was in these times that we reverted to the casual dishpan sponge bath and hoped for a storm to blow in soon. There have been days and nights when the only way we could bathe was to visit a friend who had more conveniences than we did.

We have found that it is easy to live without resources if there is no other way. If you don't have a choice, you accept what situation exists. There is a drought season going on, and the water tables are low. Yet we observe people using water as if they had a boundless supply. If you listen to people talk about the problems of conservation, you begin to get a clear picture of the seriousness of the shortages. One man told us that if he ran out of water using his existing wells, he would dig other wells. Apparently the man knew nothing about water tables or how they work.

Living on a small island in the Pacific in a house that has no water, no electricity, and no inside facility makes a person a believer of his own power and strength. It would be well worth the investment of time and money to reroute your water system and utilize the shower and kitchen sink water by running it into a holding tank and using the water in the garden. Why continue to pour gallons and gallons of water into a septic tank? If we use a pure soap for our dish washing and clothes washing as well as our own personal body washing, the water can nourish the plant life and save many gallons each day.

The effectiveness of the system we are using for our personal survival is all the proof we need to continue our work with the system. Each of us must develop a system that works for us as individuals. If we take care of our own individual resources, the resources of the planet will take care of themselves. If nobody pollutes and everybody conserves, we have a better chance of self preservation. Ecology is not just a bumpersticker. Ecology is a way of life.

MEDICINE

Medicine is the second pressing need in any survival program. If anyone in the family is taking any medication on a daily basis, this should be provided for in your family's survival plan. Heart patients, epileptics, diabetics, ladies who take estrogen, ladies who do not wish to become pregnant. . .Anyone who depends on a store of medicine should keep an advance supply of medication on hand for an emergency. Do not store away a supply of medication. Use your regular supply, then the reserve, replacing the reserve with a fresh supply and rotating its use. This way you always have a fresh supply of reserve medication. Use this method over a period of time and soon you will have a year's supply of medicine. Always make sure you have at least two weeks supply; that is, two weeks reserve.

FOOD AND FOOD STORAGE

When you plan to store food supplies, you must be sure that the food is protected from spoilage, oxidation, insects, water damage and extremes of both heat and cold. The best temperature is 55 to 65 degrees Fahrenheit. Figure out how much space you have and gather the containers to suit the type of space. Also consider the handling of the stored containers and rotating the stockpile. Most paint supply stores carry five gallon round and square metal cans. Paint dealers will generally sell you new containers with lids on them. Many restaurants and hospitals throw away both glass and plastic jars.

Do not try to store any food in containers that have held petroleum products. The odor will be absorbed by the food and can be harmful if eaten. Remember that rats and mice will chew through plastic bags or containers. Be sure to wash all containers out with a good dishwashing detergent. Even if you do not use such products, be sure to keep them on hand to wash out storage containers. Weevils love soap residue.

WHEAT

Because of the nutritional quality of wheat, it should be the first item on your list of things to store. It is a most versatile and nutritious food as well as being a very economical source of protein.

૨ગ

Long Term Food Supply Three hundred pounds of wheat is the annual average for one adult female. A grown man will need about one hundred pounds more and a child about one hundred pounds less. Hard wheat is best to store. This wheat is also known as spring wheat, Turkey Red or Marquis. It should contain 11.5 percent protein and contain less than 10 percent moisture. If the wheat is not clean when you buy it, it must be cleaned. In order to do this, you separate all foreign matter from the kernels and put the grain into a clean, dry container for storage. There are many methods of protecting the wheat from the weevils. Eucalyptus leaves mixed in with the wheat is a great protector. Bay laurel leaves work the same way. Another way to eliminate both insect eggs and moisture is to heat whatever you are storing in a pan to 150 degrees for twenty minutes and let it cool; then store it in containers. This method also works for beans and nuts as well as grains.

Nine five-gallon cans are needed to store 300 pounds of wheat, which is an average person's yearly supply of grain. Clean all containers well with hot soapy water using a good dishwashing detergent. Now that the cans are cleaned, dry them well and drop a piece of frozen carbon dioxide about the size of a walnut into the bottom of each container and pour in the grain. The five gallon containers will hold about 33 pounds of grain. Let the lids sit loosely for about twelve hours or overnight. The dry ice evaporates into carbon dioxide (an inert gas which displaces oxygen). Now screw on the lids tightly, being sure that the evaporation is complete—or the containers will blow up. When this process is complete, the grain will be well protected. No insects are able to hatch without oxygen, and no oxidation will occur either.

Another method of protecting the grain is to use a handful of diatomaceous earth tossed in with the grain that is to be stored. This works well to protect the food. Diatomaceous earth is a desiccant to insects and may even be dusted on animals to kill fleas and mites. It may be applied to plants in the garden for pest control. It may also be used to reduce flies and odors. It is non-toxic when ingested; it is harmless to the environment and it is inexpensive.

Now that you know how to store wheat, you will have to learn how to cook it and make it into an enjoyable food. The grain can be sprouted, cooked in a double boiler or pressure cooker. Some people put the grain into a thermos, filling it with hot water and letting it sit overnight. The next day the grain is ready to use as a cereal. We like to eat the cereal with a little wheat germ sprinkled over the top, a little honey and fruit (if you've got it). It is a very good source of protein and the more whole food you put on it the more food value you take into your body.

Many people feel that by having a food mill to grind the wheat you can increase your standard of survival by 500 percent. If you have a grinder, you can grind your flour for bread, cracked wheat, mush for babies, and many other dishes. Wheat could become very boring as a diet to survive on. We must learn to cook interesting dishes out of the foods we are storing and using daily.

For so many years people thought that health foods and natural wholesome foods were the pills and powders they saw on many store shelves. Health foods and health products have become very popular and the words have been exploited by anyone wanting to join the commercial bandwagon. We knew a man who made the most delicious Granola in his very nice factory. As he mixed the ingredients, he puffed on his cigarette. His office was an area of clutter. Still he preached the message of organic and natural foods.

SURVIVAL FOODS

Brewer's Yeast
Honey
Wheat
Yogurt
Powdered milk
Love
Cider vinegar
Soy beans

Stay healthy, stay happy...Work at your own pace...Find your own balance.

CHAPTER 24

ECOLOGY IS MORE THAN A BUMPERSTICKER

The crusade toward developing an ecological balance has made many advancements in the past fifteen years. The return to nature and the simple pleasures of life has brought about many eyesores. As we travel the highways and hike through the countryside, we can see clear messages of a movement to develop an awareness of preserving what is almost a dying planet. As we hike the area of the San Juan Canyon, we walk upon beer cans, styrofoam cups, plastic bottle tops, flip-top beer openers and wine bottles, as well as filter-cigarette butts. As we observe the city folks moving into the countryside, we see them establishing homes in an effort to escape the "rat race." As they move from the nearby cities, they bring with them their city ways. Some of them have had little experience living in the country. Many of them have given up their weekend cottages at the sea and replaced their summer hide-aways with a return to nature. As the canyon becomes more populated with people who have a desperate need to live a simple life of simple pleasure, the canyon becomes cluttered with plastic garbage pails, plastic hoses, and C.B. radios. As the city people move to the suburbs, they bring with them most of their city concepts.

In an effort to educate people who return to the land, we risk our own personal survival. Instead of walking through the meadows to hunt mushrooms and wild flowers, we are engaging in a crusade to educate the newcomers in survival concepts that might save their lives as well as the natural beauty of the canyon. As the cities become more populated, as the crime rates go up, and as the cities become almost impossible to live in, more and more people will reach out for what little space they can find in the suburbs. Through the message of this book we hope, at least, to present an alternative to the existing methods of survival. Today survival is more than a message. Today more than ever, survival is man's most important aim. In order to deal with the ever-rising changes, we must adapt new concepts of living. As we learn to deal with the ever-rising food costs and obvious food shortages, we learn about survival methods that will enable us to live happier and healthier lives.

For many years, scientists have questioned the survival of this planet. It has not been so many years since we first head the words "ecology" and "ecologist." When we first began to question our contribution to the ecological balance, we were surprised to find obvious imbalance. We re-examined and re-evaluated the way in which we lived. We soon realized that we were not thinking of the balance that must continue between nature and man if the planet is to exist in the future. We have studied and incorporated the ways and means of survival which promote a good ecological balance for our families.

Health foods, natural foods, organic living—what do these words mean to our survival on this planet? As we examine the environment, we see that the possibility of the planet's existence becomes more and more questionable. As teachers, we are confronted with many disagreements. We can well understand why some of the confusion would classify us, who believe in the necessity of balance, as crackpots or food faddists.

Ten years ago when many people spoke out towards the possibility of altering their lifestyles, they were called "nuts." Today, as the ecological problems of the planet become more evident, the "nuts" have become the teachers of survival. The survival message is valid to all of us living and breathing on this planet.

The fuel shortage of 1975 opened up many doors to the possibility of re-examining our lifestyles and altering them to suit the available resources. As the fuel shortages continue, many people have given up and are back to their old style of buying big cars and burning fuel needlessly. Many people are building houses without considering the high cost of maintaining them. People are building houses without thought to the amount of fuel it will take to heat the homes. Today solar energy is being considered by many people who are planning to build family home structures. The sun has become the only reliable source of comfort and heat.

It makes little sense to build a home without considering the position of the sun in relation to the placement of the home. You can get heat to any area if you take into consideration the potential of using the sun as a means of heat. The expense of utilizing solar heat is well worth the energy as the system pays for itself in a matter of a few years. There are many consultants who are eager to introduce methods and techniques of solar heating. We highly recommend that anyone building a new home in today's world consult an expert who has been trained in the field of solar energy.

As we observe the number of large cars in the area, we realize that many people do not have a good sense of real ecological balance. As we listen to people speak up in defense of developing a sensible ecological balance, we observe their actions. We question the ecology stickers on the large dirty cars. As the fossil fuels become more scarce, not even the super rich can afford to buy large cars that require large amounts of gas to operate. Money has become no object. Today we must consider the long range survival plan of the future. The necessity of balance has become obvious. Balance is the key word towards our survival plan. Education is part of the survival plan. Without knowledge there can be no survival. Knowledge is the most important commodity. Without knowledge we cannot survive. After being students of survival we will all become teachers of the most important subject ever taught—*Survival*.

Health foods and natural foods all mean plain good nutrition. One very important factor we must consider when examining our nutritional intake is individual need. We are all individuals and our needs will not be the same. If a food does not agree with you, don't eat it. Modern man has created his suffering by destroying his foods just as he has upset the natural balance in nature by polluting the environment. Man has made only destructive assaults on food in his attempt at food technology in the past 200 years. Food refining and processing, polluting the foods with sprays and changing the foods with chemical additives that deceive the consumer, have been faults which may be hard to change. Today we see food items in our markets which should not be classified as foods because they contain little or no food value. Waste and ignorance are two leading factors holding us back from the balance necessary for survival. Convenience foods are becoming more and more the style of many people in the kitchen. The foods which are of the highest nutritional value are the most time-consuming to prepare.

As we turn to new methods and techniques in our changing lifestyle, we learn to re-examine our old ways. We learn to change as the necessity for change becomes obvious. In developing a system that will work, man needs to consider his goals on a long term basis. Today passes and yesterday's methods need to be revised. Hope for the future existence of the planet is the number one factor that we must consider while developing a new system for the future of mankind living on the planet. Tomorrow can be forever if man has the determination to alter his ways.

CHAPTER 25

RETURN TO THE FAMILY

I n these times of economic crisis and ecological unrest, many people are returning to the family as a potential means of rest and relaxation from the day to day worries and cares of living in society. To many people, the home has become a source of comfort and pleasure.

Today there is a trend towards women's return to the kitchen. The women's liberation movement is still creating new worlds for those women who need banners and flags in order to feel like liberated women! Many women have become bored with projecting movies in blue jeans and chino shirts as a twenty-four hour a day costume. Many ladies are returning to a simple dress to waltz around the house in. As ladies begin the march back to the concept of the family, they bring with them a fresh desire to create an image of the lady of the house. For many years, women felt threatened by their desires to play house. For many women, playing house meant involving someone else. Playing house does not have to involve a husband or a father or a mother or a child. Many women are expressing a desire to play house alone and unattached! What is wrong with a young girl of nineteen going out into the world to play house? Many nineteen-year-olds go off to college or off to war!

We feel that parents must educate children on the subject of survival. If children are taught to *respect* available resources, they will not be frightened by any scarcity of resources. In our homes, we are constantly working towards teaching our children to conserve water, electricity, and heating fuels. As the children become more aware of the energy problem, they learn to deal with the environment as it exists today. Mankind has been lax in conserving natural resources.

It is possible to teach people the ways of living a simple life filled with simple pleasures. Many people are developing new survival systems as well as changing their attitudes towards the necessities of life. Food, shelter, love, and lots of hope have been the necessities in our homes for many years. Teaching children is insurance that they will grow up with the knowledge and information that will contribute to the ecological structure of the planet. With each generation, there is a greater drain on available resources.

There will probably be no end to the energy crisis and no end to the shortages of resources. The trick is for mankind to learn to prolong the available resources. We must learn to yield without resistance. We must learn to alter our lifestyles in order to make ourselves more comfortable with what we have available.

Developing self-sufficiency and building a family unit that can work together has been a full time project. "Mother has spoken" has been the final word on many proposals...We are learning to treat each moment as if it were the first moment of our lives. We have learned to treat our men like we did when we first met, with respect and admiration, with a strong knowledge of the fact that they have broader shoulders and probably can stand a little leaning on. We understand that we must allow our families the opportunity to act out their roles as adults, children, and parents...

As two separate women coordinating two separate homes, we know it is not the quantity of time we spend together as a family unit that counts. It is the *quality* of the time that makes us feel good about living. Through our years of experience we have discovered that some people have a direct route from their heads to their sexual centers. What is lost is their heart. We are wondering why people can't enjoy being free to live a civilized sensible life within the family unit. Everything is either positive or negative. We feel the family unit is the most positive force on the planet

As we review the possibilities of human destiny, we see that human destiny is determined by what goes on inside the skull when the human is confronted with what goes on outside the skull. Freedom gives any person the power to carry out his or her own designs. Each member of the family unit has the power and the freedom to interfere with the designs of others.

Within our family unit we eliminate lots of stress by starting from scratch each day. We develop the habit of filing yesterday away in a tape, bringing the tape out as a reference and source of information. Sometimes, simply by finding out what it is that each member of the family wants, you can work more effectively. Family meetings help to clear the air when no other messages seem to get through. When we find ourselves bored with our old habits, we change them, we develop new ones.

We like working together each day, most of the time. When the family home becomes too small, we sometimes go off into the hills to figure out why we have become tired of one another. The home is a place where we can relax when we are together. We are creating a base or home station where we can work effectively as a family unit when we are together.

We have learned not to act in a moment of haste, rather to go on letting what will go wrong, go wrong and letting it gel. We have discovered that teenagers and children, as well as adults, all want attention *when* they want it. With our boys we have found that most men are boys until they reach the age of forty, so we might as well relax and let them act out. People are who they want to be. We make no attempts to change our children. We have come to the conclusion that the children as well as the adults change when they want to change with little help from anyone!

We feel that helping the child develop his own self esteem is probably the best gift a parent can give to a child. We feel certain that happiness within the family unit is making the most of the basic necessities contained within the family structure. When our hair becomes long and shaggy, and the neighbors are looking at us like we might be mad scientists, we decide to stick to our efforts with survival concepts and carry on a little while longer. The home becomes a place where we can nourish the body, uplift the spirit, and renew the heart together.

CHAPTER 26

HOUSEHOLD RECYCLING
OR
CREATIVE GARBAGE

We are changing our habits in order to conserve energy. There are many ways to conserve energy in purchasing household necessities. Household tools and houseware items can be purchased at flea markets, garage sales, and second hand stores rather than at stores that sell only new items. For many years we have encouraged our friends to shop in second hand stores. We buy most of our clothing, housewares, and tools along with records and books in used stores.

One of man's primary goals must be to change his daily habits of living. For centuries, man has taken from the natural resources of the planet. Now that depletion of our natural resources is obvious, man must return to his old way of living in order to conserve the exisiting natural resources. As time passes, we are becoming more aware of the problems of ecological imbalance. There are many items in second hand stores which can be purchased at a savings compared to the high prices of new stores. One only has to accustom oneself to shopping for used items. After one develops the habit of making a list of the necessary items and setting one day aside to shop and "tour" the used shops, shopping becomes easy, economical, and fun. We have been able to purchase many items at bargain prices simply by waiting until we find what we need in used stores rather than rushing out to purchase these items in new shops. We have been able to find everything from a warm winter coat to used candles in our "favorite shops." This also eliminates any need for time payment or purchases on credit. Another step towards self sufficiency.

We must change our patterns of living during these times of economical and ecological crisis. We have eliminated all of the paper towels and napkins from our shopping lists. We have replaced these items by sewing napkins out of scrap or remnant materials. In most supermarkets where you shop for your family's food supply, you are surrounded by "convenience" items. Most of these products create garbage and waste. Disposable diapers cannot be recycled. Do not buy items which add to the mountain of garbage being produced by modern man.

We see items such as paper napkins, towels, plates, and cups as completely unnecessary for survival. Paper is made from trees. Trees are a valuable resource, not to be wasted on man's lazy habits of living.

We try not to throw any item away. We remember the habits of our grandmothers. "What you don't need today you may need tomorrow." Grandma used to save everything from string to Grandpa's old shoes. Once the shoe leather was beyond repair, she would cut holes in the shoe soles in order to use the shoes as a planter. A pair of boots worn and aged by a special friend can become charming and interesting conversation pieces in any home. In times when there was plenty of money to spend on such frivolity, people used to bronze baby shoes. Today many people are using the shoes as pin holders and vases rather than spending the time and energy on bronze.

We must learn to save plastic bags and containers. We have used paper bags until they are ready to fall apart. After we have collected a large supply of bags, we sometimes end up carrying the bags to the shops and requesting that the shop keeper put our commodities in them rather than using new bags. At one time we used to get questioned on this habit. Today, because shop owners are faced with high overhead, they realize the savings this habit allows.

The best approach towards conservation is the elimination of waste. If you have a fireplace or wood-burning stove, it makes no sense to throw your old newspapers and junk mail in the garbage can. Use them for starting your fires. Milk cartons and other cardboard items also make good fire starters.

The leftovers in your refrigerator can be used to prepare new and imaginative dishes. As a last resort, you can feed them to your cats and dogs.

Vegetable trimmings, egg shells, and all biodegradable items can be put to work. We have an old diaper pail in our kitchen which now has the grand title of "slop bucket." All of our kitchen waste goes into the bucket. Once a day it is emptied into the compost pile. Our leaves, prunings and weeds from the yard also go into the compost. A compost pile can be made in any unused corner of your property. It can be dug into the ground and camouflaged so no one even knows it's there. As you add your kitchen and garden wastes, throw a little dirt in with it, some manure if you have it; just make sure it is all biodegradable, that it will decompose naturally. Your decomposed garbage makes excellent fertilizer after it has gone through the composting procedure and will help you produce better plants in your garden naturally.

We try to eliminate plastic bottles, boxes, etc. in our shopping carts. Plastic is hard to recycle. Burning it produces poisonous fumes which pollute the air. Melted plastic makes a nasty mess in your fireplace. Plastic is not biodegradable; it can lay buried in the earth for thousands of years and still retain its total ugliness. Plastic is made from petroleum; oil is becoming scarce and is needed for other uses.

Plastic bags are very much a part of modern packaging. It is foolish to buy new plastic bags when you can get an ample supply free from the items you purchase in the supermarket. Plastic bags can be used over and over again. If we wash the bags out and dry them, they will be clean and fresh for future use.

Many items are packaged in plastic tubs with tight-fitting plastic lids. These containers can be used for many things around the house.

Glass is made from natural elements and can easily be recycled. Many large cities have places where you can take your glass for recycling. We have one garbage can for glass. All the glass is broken as we put it in the can so it takes up less room.

Aerosol cans are another "no-no." Most products that come in aerosol cans can be purchased in different packaging material. There is a great awareness today of the gases put into our atmosphere by aerosol cans. Many scientists believe these gases are destroying the ozone layer in the stratosphere above the planet.

Many tin cans can and should be recycled. Aluminum containers can be turned in to a recycling center where they will pay you a good sum. Most aluminum recycling centers request that you bring in only crushed aluminum. Stomping aluminum cans is an excellent way to vent frustrations.

Today we are finding it necessary and fun to return to the frugal methods of the early pioneers. It is necessary to become a "jack of all trades" in order to live in today's world. You say you don't know how to become a person who can make an old thing over into a new thing? Nonsense—every person is creative.

Many families and organizations make projects out of collecting aluminum cans and returnable bottles from the sides of highways and country roads. We are for this 100 percent. We cringe as we drive along the roads and see all the unclaimed garbage lying in neglected piles. "One way" bottles, disposable diapers, cigarette butts and wrappers, tin cans, wine bottles, etc. All the flotsam and jetsam of civilization—garbage put on display to decorate America by careless, thoughtless, lazy people. Enough said. "Don't throw it away" is our motto.

CHAPTER 27

MICHAEL F. COOK'S LIVING WITH THE SUN

Imagine a house that has no access to wood, gas, electricity, coal, or oil—and yet still requires heat. If we were asked to heat it under such circumstances, the simplest answer would be with the sun's direct energy. The simplicity and effectiveness of solar heating makes it a necessary tool for anyone concerned with self-sufficiency. With inevitable shortages and rising costs of conventional fuels, it makes good sense to plan around these problems by plugging directly into the sun.

There are many strategies and levels of technology used to trap the sun's energy. This guide is intended to introduce those methods that are applicable without the use of complex hardware.

The concepts offered herein were known in their more rudimentary forms to the Incas, Greeks, Aztecs, Romans, and just about any other civilization that thought the sun to be of importance. What we will be doing is rediscovering the nearly-lost art of solar tempering, which is the process by which we make structures thermally tolerable to their occupants.

If we are to be successful in utilizing the sun's energy for heating we must understand four concepts involved in any solar scheme. We must:

1. Understand the path of the sun in relation to us;
2. Comprehend methods of actually capturing sunshine;
3. Learn to store excess heat; and,
4. Realize the overriding importance of insulation and good solar design.

SOLAR PATHS

The sun rises in the east and sets in the west. As it passes each day from east to west, it is always to the south of us (in the United States). As a result of this fact, we are best able to trap the sun's energy by orienting our homes toward the south, where the sun strikes much of the day.

Depending upon the season of the year, the actual altitude of the sun in the sky varies. In winter, the sun sits low in the sky, and in the summer, it is much higher.

This is convenient in the sense that we can size our overhangs to keep the extremely strong summer sun out and still allow winter sun to strike below the overhangs when the sun's warmth is most needed.

THE WINDOW AS A COLLECTOR

Since the discovery of glass, man has been able to allow heat and light in without having to pay utility companies for the sun's services. Unfortunately, with the discovery and use of fossil fuels, windows no longer serve their functions as heaters and illuminators but instead have most often become "picture" windows, oblivious to orientation and consequently usefulness.

Few people realize the tremendous heating potential of south-facing windows. The reason we have begun our discussion of solar collection with windows is because they *are* the easiest, cheapest, and as far as we are concerned, the best way of heating our homes.

GREENHOUSES

Another approach to warming a cold home involves incorporating a greenhouse into the design. Greenhouses admit a substantial amount of light and maintain high temperatures during the daylight hours. If we design our homes to utilize this heat and store the excess, we will be far ahead financially and materially of those who must go out and buy expensive and complex heating hardware.

TROMBE WALL

Some people are made uncomfortable by direct sunlight, and others may not desire a greenhouse. For those individuals, there is a third low-cost alternative. The "Trombe wall" involves most often a south-facing masonry wall, painted black, and then enclosed with glass, allowing a gap (4 to 7 inches) between the wall and its covering to facilitate air movement. By placing vents at the top and bottom of the wall equal to roughly 5 percent of the glass-enclosed area, a natural circulation will occur when the sun shines. Hot air rises through the top vent and into the house, while cooler air from the inside of the house meanders through the bottom port to be reheated and recycled into the house. During the summer, if you live in an area that has cool nights, the vents can be left open and the air cycle will reverse, naturally cooling the interior.

In using windows, greenhouses, and Trombe walls for heating, it is important to remember that during nights and cloudy periods, it is important to insulate these areas from the rest of the house because they experience enormous heat losses.

The aforementioned natural heating systems are those that should be employed when possible. They require the least energy in construction, maintenance and materials.

For older homes with little structural flexibility, it is often difficult to incorporate natural heat gain systems. In these situations, flat plate collectors become useful because of their placement flexibility (roof, ground, away from house.) A flat plate solar collector consists of an insulated box (wood or metal usually) a solar absorber plate (metal, plastic, glass) and a top covering of glass or plastic. The collector is oriented south for maximum winter heat. As the sun strikes the absorber plate, it gets hot. This heat is then transported off the absorber plate to the house, or to storage, by water running over the plate, or in tubes bonded to the plate, or by air blown over the plate. In systems that employ water as the transport medium, the storage consists most often of large insulated tanks. Some tanks have been constructed large enough to heat houses through weeks of cold, cloudy weather, though most often the storage is of the one to two day type.

In systems that use air as the transfer medium, large insulated bins filled with rocks are most often used for storage.

These systems can provide for the heating needs of the home but at a much more costly material price than windows, greenhouses, and Trombe walls.

STORING HEAT

Different materials have different capacities for storing heat. Air can store very little heat without experiencing extreme temperature rises. Wood doesn't do a very good job either. Masonry however, does well, and water even better than masonry.

When we design our shelters, we should take these facts into account. If we want to be able to heat our homes mostly with the sun, we must be able to store heat for days that have no sun. In just about any solar heating system, there will come a time when some sort of auxiliary heat source will be needed. My choice is wood heat for three reasons. It is not outrageously expensive, is available in most locales, and is a recyclable energy source *if* properly managed.

BUILDING A THERMOS

We have already discussed means by which to trap and store heat. *None* of this is of much value unless we are able to retain the heat we gain within the confines of the structure. To understand the general heating requirements of the home, we must understand the various heat loss values of materials that make up the home.

Windows on east, west, and especially north faces are responsible for 30 to 50 percent of the heat losses in many U.S. homes. Windows lose heat at twelve times the rate of an average wood-framed wall containing three-and-one-half inches of fiberglass insulation. The first recommendation, then, is to limit windows, as much as possible, to the south face of the house, and insulate all windows with shutters, heavy drapes, or other means when they are not serving a useful function.

Infiltration of outside air into the home is another drain on heat supplies. Well weather-stripped doors, double doors, weather-stripped windows, double windows, and tight vents slow down hot air leakage.

The structural frame of the home must also be air tight and well insulated. Escalating prices of fuels make it nearly impossible to over-insulate.

Proper landscaping can contribute much to a home's heating efficiency. Windbreaks cut down chill factors and heat losses, while reflective ground cover on the south side of homes contributes heat indirectly to the home via windows.

In a society that most often prescribes complex answers for its problems, it is a relief to know that there remain simple solutions such as heating with the sun. Our technology, in essence our methodology, has brought us many good things.

However, it has also brought with it terms like "precision" and "efficiency" that, in some cases, are counterproductive. Trying to heat a home to exactly 68 degrees at all times has taken extreme mental and mechanical energy. Trying to make a home comfortable is a lot less difficult and frees much of our creative time to pursue solutions to truly complex problems confronting the totality of mankind.

We spend far too much time and energy making things perfect that only need to be functional, or sometimes don't need to be at all, and too little time on the things that matter. Imagine if the time, money, and mental energy expended on creating more efficient moonshots and nuclear power plants had been spent on trying to understand people's problems in getting along with one another. Imagine if $\frac{1}{1000}$th of the energy spent on the "atomic age" had been spent on designing and implementing solar systems for home and industry. Imagine it all, and then see what simple and yet meaningful contributions you can make to your life and to others.

CHAPTER 28

ONLY ONE WAY

The concept of "only one way" is to develop our potentials individually. The process of working at our own individual goals through the development of our own individual system is possible. Our own personal motivation is the force that drives us towards developing our own individual system of survival. Health and happiness, along with the ability to deal with the changing environment, are goals that each individual takes full responsibility for. As the world economic situation is ever changing, and as the natural resources are depleted, we must take a personal stand to develop a system of living that will preserve what resources we have available.

Exploring new concepts of survival and nutrition as well as developing new styles of control of the environment has become a way of life for many people. Learning to deal with the environment is an art. Today survival is everybody's business. In order to survive we must develop our own system of survival—or we will not survive.

Most of us have already set our standards of living each day in health and happiness. Living each day like a rhythm has become an easy way for many of us. Many people have been able to live sensible lives in keeping with ecological balance and available resources. It is one thing to be able to go off into the hills and survive. It is quite another thing to learn to survive in a city filled with distractions. Webster's definition of survival is, "To live longer; to outlive or outlast; to remain alive." Survival does not mean back to the land. Survival doesn't mean the look of plants and pots in every tract house in America. Survival doesn't mean wild hickory nuts. Survival means staying alive longer, using and conserving the available resources. The most important goal is to develop a desire to survive and adapt a system that works for the individual.

As we evaluate our old habits of surviving, we soon forget the habits that are no longer working for us. We accept change as it occurs. We eat nutritious foods, we get plenty of rest, we drink lots of good water. We learn to appreciate the control that the mind has over the body. We learn to observe what we are actually and what we are potentially.

Everything in the universe is related. We accept what is and let go of our illusions.

We appreciate our need to develop our separate goals and work towards arriving at these goals. When we meet as a unit of people, we bring with us individual strength that is the strength of our unit. As we develop our own individual system, we enjoy the pleasures as we feel the brunt of the pain. If in the process of developing a system, we find it impossible to work within the system, we discover the alternatives. At last, when all else seems to fail, we can catch a tortoise going south and hope that we can arrive at our destiny in time to enjoy a few years of clean air and simple living.

ADDITIONAL READING

SPROUTS AND HOW TO GROW AND EAT THEM—Alice Muller

DIET FOR A SMALL PLANET—Frances Moore Lappé

CONFESSIONS OF A SNEAKY ORGANIC COOK—Kinderleader

TEN TALENTS—Hurd

BACK TO EDEN—Kloss, Jethro

FROM EDEN TO AQUARIUS—Greig Brodsky

THE WHOLE EARTH COOKBOOK—Sharon Cadwallader, Judi Ohr

IN CELEBRATION OF SMALL THINGS—Sharon Cadwallader

TASSAJARA BREAD BOOK—Brown, Edward Espe

HOW TO PREPARE FOR THE COMING CRASH—Robert Preston

VITAL FOODS FOR TOTAL HEALTH—Benard Jensen

EARTH WATER FIRE AIR—Barbara Freiedander

THE HERB BOOK—John Lust

SOLAR HOME BOOK—Bruce Anderson

DIRECT USE OF THE SUN'S ENERGY—Farrington Danials

SOLAR ENERGY UTILIZATION FOR HEATING AND
    COOLING—John Yellot

SUN SPOTS—Steve Baer

AN INTRODUCTION TO THE USE OF THE WIND—
    Douglas Coonley

ENERGY FOR SURVIVAL—Wilson Clark

ENERGY PRIMER—Portola Institute, 1974

NEW LOW COST SOURCES OF ENERGY FOR THE HOME—
    Peter Klegg

OTHER HOMES AND GARBAGE—Jim Leckie and others, 1975

SCIENTIFIC AMERICAN MAGAZINE

THE SAVORY WILD MUSHROOM—Margaret McKenny

A FIELD GUIDE TO WESTERN MUSHROOMS—
    Alexander H. Smith

SHELTERS, SHACKS AND SHANTIES—D. C. Beard

HOMEMADE HOUSES—Art Boericke and Barry Shapiro

INDEX

Note: Recipes are indicated by page numbers in boldface type.

Spaghetti, garlic, **93**
Spearmint, 27
Speech, herbs for loss of, 27
Spinach,
    frittata, **91**
    in ravioli, 92
Spread, liver, **88**
Sprouting,
    method of, 73–74
    seeds for, 15
Sprouts, 73–75
    bean, salad of, **78, 80**
    burgers, **90**
    and eggplant enchiladas, **76**
Squares, crunchy sesame, **114**
Squash, blossoms of, 29
Squid sauce, **83**
Stock, basic soup, **65–67**
Strawberry, 27
    pie, **104**
St. John's wort, 27
Sugar,
    date, with wheat germ, 19
    powdered, 111
    raw, 10
    substituting honey for, 11
    turbinado, 10
Sunflower seed / s,
    in candy, 108, 109
    in cookies, 113
    cracked, 15
    in granola, 95
    for indoor greens, 75
    loaf, **98**
    meal, 15
    roasted, salted, 15
    and soy flour bread, **41**
Sun. *See* Energy, solar
Survival, 127–29, 130
    planning for, 119–25
Sweet peas, 30

Tahini, 10
Tansy, 27
Tapioca, 14
Tea, herbal, to make, **21**. *See also individual herbs*
Thermos,
    building a house as, 138–39
    cooking wheat in, 124
Thyme, 27
Tofu (soy bean curd), 60
    cheese cake, **63**
    loaf, baked, **61**
    in pie, 60
    scrambled, **62**
Toilet, saving water use in, 121
Tomato / es,
    canned,
        for enchiladas, 76
        in sauce, 83
        soup of, 71
    fresh,
        in salad, 79
        in salsa, 82
    juice, 98
    paste,
        with rabbit, 87
        in sauce, 83
    in sauce, 82
    soup, with cashews, **71**
Topping, for carrot cake, **110**
Tortillas,
    corn, 76, 88
    flour, 88
    whole wheat, **98**

Triticale,
    flour, 14
    whole, 18
Trombe wall, 137

Vegetables, for chicken soup, 67
Vervain, 27
Violets, 27, 28
    candied, **29**
Vitamins, natural, 7

Walnuts,
    in cake, 112
    in cookies, 114
    in rolls, 99
Water,
    to can, 120
    conservation of, 119–22
    to store, 119–20
Watercress, 26
    salad, **80**
Water system, planned, 120
Wheat, 19
    berries, 19
        in bread, 39, 40
    bulgur. *See* Bulgur
    to clean, 124
    cracked, bread of, **46**
    flakes, 19
        in cereal, 94
    flour,
        unbleached,
            hard, 14, 15, 38
            soft (pastry), 14
        whole, 15
            in bread, 39, 40, 49
    germ. *See* Wheat germ
    for indoor greens, 75
    milk, 75
    rolled, in bread, 39
    for sprouting, 73, 74–75, 124
    to store, 123–24
    whole, 10, 15, 39, 40, 49
    tortillas, **98**
Wheat germ, 10, 19
    in bread, 38, 39, 41, 49, 98
    and carob chip pie, **105**
    in cereal, 94, 95
    in cookies, 114
    in mocksa balls, 67
    in pancakes, 96
    for pie crust, 63
    in quick bread, 101
Window, as a solar collector, 136

Yeast,
    cake, 37
    dry, 37
    nutritional, in drink, 56
    quantities needed, 37
    to store, 37
Yerba santana, 27
Yogurt, 11, 53–56
    drink, **54, 55, 56**
    to make, **53**
    salad dressing, **54**
    in soup, 72
    soup of, cold, **55**

Zucchini,
    casserole, **90**
    pancakes, **97**

147

OTHER BOOKS OF INTEREST FROM CELESTIAL ARTS...

THE SACRED LANDSCAPE, by Fredric Lehrman. Full-color photographs of the most sacred spots on earth—areas of striking beauty and power that have been seen through the ages as special. 128 pages, oversize; $27.95 paperback; $49.95 clothbound; $100.00 deluxe boxed edition.

LOVING THE EARTH, by Fredric Lehrman, Illustrated by Lisa Tune. A collection of stunning artwork and photos with easy-to-read text to teach children about the wonderful planet we live on. 48 pages, oversize; $17.95 clothbound.

JOURNEYS ON MIND MOUNTAIN, by G. BlueStone. These nature essays serve to calm the mind and stir the spirit with their meditative look at the wonders of the natural world. 144 pages; $7.95 paperback.

THE ART OF RITUAL, by Renee Beck and Sydney Barbara Metrick. A guide to creating and performing personalized rituals for growth and change, this book shows you how to make up your own rituals for any significant event in your life. 192 pages; $11.95 paperback.

PRAYERS OF SMOKE, by Barbara Means Adams. A Native American descendant of Black Elk presents fundamental beliefs of the Makaha tribe, including creation stories, myths, and symbology. 172 pages; $9.95 paperback.

THE DAY THE WORLD FORGOT, by Robert Skutch. This short novel speaks simply yet powerfully to the human yearning for peace beyond all ideologies, all political divisions, and all national and religious boundaries. 80 pages; $8.95 clothbound.

THESE BOOKS AVAILABLE AT YOUR LOCAL BOOKSTORE
OR DIRECT FROM CELESTIAL ARTS.
Call or write for details.

CELESTIAL ARTS
Post Office Box 7327 • Berkeley, California 94707 • (415) 524-1801